BACK TO BASICS

How the Eight Basics of Kaizen Based
Lean Manufacturing™ turned a
Failing Manufacturing Plant
into a Success Story

A Business Novel

Bill Gaw

Founder and President

Business Basics, LLC

CGW
PUBLISHING

2013

BACK TO BASICS

How the Eight Basics of Kaizen Based Lean Manufacturing™ turned a Failing Manufacturing Plant into a Success Story

Bill Gaw

First Edition: April 2013

ISBN 978-1-908239-26-8

Published by:

CGW Publishing
B 1502
PO Box 15113
Birmingham
B2 2NJ
United Kingdom

www.cgwpublishing.com

mail@cgwpublishing.com

Contents

Chapter One

The Unfortunate and Needless Failure of Tommy, a Plant Manager One Year on the Job

Pete, corporate vice president of operations and Tommy's boss, sighed and shook his head. "Face it, Tommy, your entire operation is becoming unglued."

As painful as it was to admit, Tommy knew Pete was right. And it disheartened him. He felt as depressed right now, this instant, as he had ever felt in his entire life. But he knew he had to hide it. Three years as a Marine Corps infantry officer after college and another ten years in the management ranks of corporate America had taught him to hide his feelings, his disappointments, and keep on plugging away. As that once-famous Timex ad had stated: Takes a licking and keeps on ticking.

Pete said, "Let's take a look at the record of your plant over the past year."

Tommy took a deep breath and girded himself for the inevitable ass-eating. "Fire away, Pete." As soon as the words tumbled out of his mouth he realized his mistake, and hastily added, "I'm listening." He straightened in his chair, hoping Pete wasn't going to take his slip of the tongue literally.

Frankly, he was concerned, even a little frightened. They were in Pete's office at corporate headquarters 90 miles away from Tommy's plant, Pete behind his desk, and Tommy perched in front of it on a solitary hard-backed wooden chair. The inquisition chair as he and his peers called it.

The placement of the chair was ominous. On the occasions that Pete summoned the company's four plant managers to his office he usually had them sit on the long sofa in the corner while he sat on a leather chair adjacent to them. He sat behind his desk only when he had bad news to dispense. Not a good way to kick off Friday afternoon in Tommy's book. Another bad sign: Employees get the axe on Fridays.

"I don't know where to start." Pete hesitated for a moment to gather his thoughts. "Let's begin with my impressions, and then discuss facts and figures."

Tommy's heartbeat jumped from second to third, then into overdrive.

"First off," Pete said, "I used to enjoy touring your plant whenever I visited. I looked forward to exchanging small talk with the supervisors and workers. Guys and gals who have worked for the company for many years... I don't get that enjoyment anymore."

Tommy stared at his shoes.

"Want to know why?"

Tommy really didn't but managed to croak a yes.

"The plant is cluttered. You can't walk down an aisle without tripping over a parts container. And, damn it, parts don't belong in the aisles. You know that. They should be either in staging areas or designated storage areas or in locked cribs. Same criticism goes for the assembly area. Parts lying everywhere.

"Which brings up the subject of inventory. Your inventory turn rate sucks. It's dropping, and that's no wonder. The plant is choking with parts everywhere you look - in machining, assembly, and finished goods. Never seen so much inventory."

"I - "

Pete wasn't about to be interrupted. "The last physical inventory showed a loss. Meaning you've either lost control of inventory or your burden rate was calculated too high for the year and you've got a shitload of unabsorbed burden. In my opinion, you've got both problems... And unabsorbed burden goes right to the bottom line as a loss." Pete swore under his breath.

Tommy was afraid to say anything.

"The machining departments are filthy. We put a lot of money into cleaning them up last year, and we're now back where we started. Oil and rags all over the place. A safety hazard."

Tommy kept staring at his shoes as if they were the most fascinating objects in the world. He inwardly winced as his boss continued to work up a head of steam. Not the most patient guy in the world.

"Another thing that pisses me off. I notice a lot of workers idling around as if there isn't enough work to do."

"We're short on parts, Pete. It's always been that way. My predecessor had the same problem."

Pete snorted. "Short on parts? With all the parts you've got lying around? Give me a break."

"I should have said, short of the right parts."

Pete rose from his chair and leaned toward Tommy, his hands braced on the desk. "Then why in hell aren't you doing something about it?"

Pete's eyes blazed, making Tommy cringe. "You're right, Pete. I haven't done enough."

"Haven't done enough? Jeez!"

Pete sat back down and closed his eyes for a moment to regain his composure. "Look, Tommy, I want to see you succeed. Hell, I hired you. But the cleanliness and the clutter I just pointed out. Do you know what they represent?"

"You told me often enough. A lack of organization and discipline."

Pete slapped his hand on the desk, making Tommy jump. "Exactly! A lack of organization and discipline. But there's another factor involved here. Your resolve to get the job done.

And Tommy, it's flagging. When you started
with the company a year ago, you were full of
piss and vinegar, but I haven't noticed any of
that lately."

Tommy remained silent.

Pete removed his glasses and rubbed his eyes.
"Okay, enough of me grousing. Let's talk
numbers."

Tommy gripped the edges of his chair.

"The quality of your shipments has been slowly
deteriorating. It wasn't anything to get alarmed
about at first. You had an action plan and I
accepted that" - Pete glared at Tommy - "but
now I wonder if the plan wasn't all smoke and
mirrors."

"It's starting to take hold"

"Don't interrupt me right now, Tommy," Pete
said in a threatening tone Tommy had never
heard before from his boss. "Returns are up five
percent for the quarter, and overall up seven
percent for the year. To make matters worse I
just had a call from Jake Smith, president of

Nebraska Automotive Supply, your largest customer. Know what he told me?"

"No, I don't," Tommy said in a low voice.

"He said what we're shipping to him recently is the worst quality he's seen in years. And I believe it, Tommy. Do you know why?"

"No, I don't."

"Because end of month time in your plant is pure bedlam. I personally witnessed it the closing days of last month. Your guys and gals running around like chickens with their heads cut off, trying to squeeze two weeks of shipments into three days. I never saw such a mess. No attention to quality whatsoever, just jamming shipments out the back door. Guess what happens to quality when it's dropped by the wayside. I don't have to tell you that, do I?"

Tommy, eyes cast down, shook his head.

"Despite that frantic activity - or maybe because of it - you're missing scheduled ship dates. And it's been getting steadily worse over the past four months. Our once sterling record of achieving 92 percent of our scheduling commitments is down the toilet. Makes us look like a bunch of goddamn school kids running the plant."

Tommy tried to slide down into his seat, but there was no place to hide and no escaping Pete's wrath. The more Pete talked, the angrier he became. This was turning into the greatest ass chewing of all time. Tommy feared for his job.

Pete abruptly rose and walked to the window overlooking the parking lot below and stared outside until he cooled off. He returned to his desk and plopped into his chair as if he had just run a marathon. "I could go on and on. I could talk about excessive overtime, a drop in labor productivity, the new MRP[1] system spewing out tons of garbage information, lots of other things. Instead, let me ask you, Tommy, what in hell is going wrong?"

---

1 Materials Requirement Planning. A computerized system of scheduling goods through the plant while (ideally) maintaining inventory at minimum levels.

Tommy took a deep breath. "Look, I can give you a dozen reasons why things are as screwed up as they are now, but I won't. It's my responsibility, I understand that. Maybe I shouldn't have let the IS[2] people talk me into installing the MRP system. It looked promising at the time."

"That's just one of the problems."

"What can I say? Other than to let you know I do recognize the problems and I'm taking steps to correct them."

Hank leaned back in his chair and sighed. "It's not enough, Tommy. I've already decided on a course of action."

Tommy froze. The color drained from his face.

Pete noticed Tommy's reaction. "Ease up. It's not what you think it is. I'm not firing you. You're getting one more chance. I recognize you're new on the job and you've got a lot to learn."

---

2 Information Systems. The function responsible for implementing, compiling and disseminating data, including the MRP system.

Tommy almost sighed with relief.

"Remember Hank, the lean manufacturing consultant?"

"Sure, who hasn't? He was the consultant who turned around our Alhambra plant several years ago."

"That's right. Ten years ago to be exact, when I was plant manager there. I've stayed in touch with him over the years, and asked him yesterday to take a look at your problems and make recommendations that will get your plant back on track. Lucky for you, Hank agreed."

"I heard comments that he was retiring."

"Not true. He doesn't keep the same backbreaking workload he once kept, but like a lot of successful consultants, he doesn't know when to quit. He's having too much fun, and besides he's just in his middle fifties. Lucky for us. He's one of the early practitioners of lean manufacturing practices in the USA and arguably one of the most successful."

"Am I hearing right? You're going to get Hank, the lean manufacturing consultant, to take a look at my operations and help me?" Tommy's voice rose with excitement.

"That's exactly what I said. As a personal favor to me. You'll like him. He's a roll-up-your-sleeves guy. No theory, no bullshit. Just get the job done, and believe me, he gets to the point without any wasted time. At times, he can be blunt. But a tough ex-Marine like you can handle it. Actually, you two should get along quite well."

"I appreciate this break, Pete."

"I'm glad, Tommy" - Pete leaned forward and his voice turned icy - "but make no mistake about it. You either make this work or you pack your bags."

Chapter Two

Trouble at Home

Every time Tommy unlocked and opened the front door of his custom-built five bedroom house in the town's most upscale subdivision, he pictured dollars flying away on imaginary wings. Mortgage payment, taxes, lawn service, fashionable clothes for his wife (the woman was a clothes hog), daily maid service, grand vacations, and upkeep for his wife's Mercedes, along with every other imaginable expense needed to maintain a posh life style. Thankfully the company provided him with a fully loaded Buick Enclave and country club membership. Those additional expenses would have pushed him over the edge. Still, he was living on the brink of financial ruin and he knew it. It gnawed away at him in private moments.

His whole extravagant lifestyle was in peril now. For the first time in his life he was coming to the painful realization that he was living over his head. Way over his head. It took the shock of facing sudden unemployment to shake the tree.

He didn't know whether or not to tell his wife, Jerri, about his work problems. She was more addicted to high living than he was, and the woman had never shown any interest in

Tommy's work beyond the dollar amount of his paycheck. Foolishly, he had done nothing to discourage her profligate spending.

Jerri's father, a roughshod former small-time gambler with mob connections, was one of those roll-up-your sleeve entrepreneurs who parlayed a small sports-betting parlor in Las Vegas into a large bookie operation, some of that business legal, much of it illegal. Rumor had it he knew how to break legs when a patron reneged on his debt.

He had married a Las Vegas showgirl and Jerri was his only child. He showered his precious baby girl with utter devotion and spoiled her beyond reason as she grew older. Private schools, flashy cars, stylish clothing, overpriced jewelry, everything that a truckload of money could buy.

When Tommy and Jerri married five years ago, her father threw a wedding bash at Bellagio, one of Las Vegas's most upscale hotels, with over 500 guests in attendance, many of them mob-connected, all of them spending lavishly on wedding gifts for Tommy and Jerri.

Tommy's wife was accustomed to the finest, demanded it as her due, and her father expected Tommy to provide the same lifestyle for his daughter. Tommy, a cocky young industrial engineer with a metals product company and a bright future at the time of their wedding, didn't think twice about his ability to handle the burden, For the first four years of his marriage, while he was climbing his way up the corporate ladder, Jerri's father contributed to their support so they could live well beyond their means. But once Tommy was hired in his new position as plant manager last year the contributions stopped, and the burden transferred to his shoulders.

Tommy came from a hardscrabble background, a single child in a hasty marriage that came about when his father, on leave and drunk, impregnated his pretty mother and decided, hell, why not get married? He sure could do worse. A career enlisted man in the Navy, he seldom came home after the marriage, missed his son's birth, and only occasionally contributed money to the family's household. After serving twenty years in the Navy most of it in on the high seas and in foreign ports, he retired and abandoned his family to shack up with a sixteen-year-old Mexican girl in Cabo San Lucas at the southern tip of Baja Mexico. Tommy never saw or heard from his old man after his sixth birthday.

Tommy's mother, a factory worker in a Patterson, New Jersey lamp factory, barely made ends meet, although Tommy had to admit she denied him nothing as he was growing up. He finished high school, graduated from Rutgers with a business degree, and joined the Marine Corps, attending officer candidate school at Quantico, Virginia. After receiving his commission and the gold bars that accompanied it, he was stationed at Camp Pendleton, California, and later served one tour of duty in Afghanistan.

***

"This isn't happening," Jerri said, and nervously lit a cigarette. A one-cigarette a day smoker, Jerri betrayed her anxiety by lighting her second cigarette of the day, barely an hour after she smoked the first.

"There's no reason to panic," Tommy said. "I still have a chance to come out of this in good shape."

"A chance? Just a chance? That's pitiful."

A tall brunette, Jerri had a knockout figure conditioned by tennis matches, daily gym workouts, and rigid dieting. In the looks department she was the dazzling beauty her showgirl mother had once been. But temperamentally, she had inherited her father's volatile and nasty disposition.

Tommy and Jerri had no children because Jerri didn't want pregnancy to mar her lithe figure. That became a major point of contention in the marriage, since Tommy badly desired a couple of kids. But, as usual, what Jerri wanted, Jerri got.

Tommy sighed. "I probably shouldn't have told you about the conversation with my boss."

Jerri's eyes spit fire. "Tommy, look at me. You damn well better keep me informed. I'm your wife and partner and, damn it, I share in the decision making."

"Don't I know it," Tommy grumbled under his breath.

"If you had been more like my dad, this never would have happened."

Tommy winced. "Yeah, sure, your wonderful dad."

Jerri scowled. "Bet your ass, my wonderful dad! The same guy who supported us for four years."

"He didn't support us, he supported your expensive lifestyle. And I'm getting really sick of you throwing your father in my face. You do it whenever you're upset and you can't face the truth."

Jerri's face turned beet red. "Can't face the truth? You ingrate. How dare you say that?"

Jerri didn't handle criticism well. Tommy knew that. Truth be known, he had been just as brash. But since his talk with Pete yesterday his confidence had deflated faster than a punctured balloon. He was in no mood to listen to his wife listing his perceived faults.

"Jerri, you can push me around so far and no further. You're knocking on the door right now. Enough is enough. Unless you don't give a damn about preserving our marriage."

"Marriage? What marriage? If you can't keep your end up and support me, there is no marriage."

"I can keep my end up all right. How about you? Does keeping your end up mean getting personal attention - and I mean personal attention - from your tennis instructor and gym trainer?"

As Jerri paled and gasped for breath, Tommy threw another coal on the fire: "I don't need your whining right now, not with the problems at work facing me."

"Enough of this shit!" Jerri crushed her cigarette in a crystal cut ashtray and spun around and stormed out of the room, leaving Tommy angry with her, but angrier with himself, wondering why he had been tough enough to tangle with fierce Afghan fighters but not tough enough to handle his wife.

Chapter Three

Tommy Meets Hank, the Lean Manufacturing Consultant, Who Explains Why Tommy's Manufacturing Operation is Failing

Monday morning after his daily 7:00 am staff meeting, Tommy found Hank, the lean manufacturing consultant, waiting in his plant office. Pictures of him didn't capture the essence of the man. Although he looked considerably younger, according to what his boss, Pete, had told him, Hank was in his middle fifties. He was also very tall. Tommy estimated him at 6"3", solidly built, with a military bearing, and a welcoming smile that could make crown princes feel welcome.

Hank's smile washed over Tommy's face as he rose to introduce himself. Despite his friendly manner he was an intimidating man, Tommy thought, because of his formidable reputation.

"Tommy, I'm Hank. Great to meet you."

They shook hands and exchanged small talk for a few minutes until Hank was reasonably sure Tommy felt at ease. He waved his hand around the office. "Is this where we will be meeting?"

"Yes sir."

"Please call me Hank. I don't stand on formality. And I'll call you... Tom or Tommy?" He had a strong Midwest accent, befitting a man who had lived most of his life in Michigan's beautiful Upper Peninsula.

"Tommy's fine."

Hank got right to it. "Tommy it is. We'll structure your manufacturing lessons around eight basics of lean manufacturing management, all of which I'll explain later. Suffice it to say for now we'll cover them one subject at a time. One hour a day or so for however many days it takes, with the final day discussing self-directed work teams."

"Is that final session one of the eight principles of lean management?"

"No, it isn't. But without self-directed work teams to carry out the tasks required by the eight basic principles, they simply won't work anywhere near as well... Anyway, getting back to our format, I'll give you homework assignments related to the day's topics and expect that you will study them every night. After we complete this introduction phase, you and I will start implementing the lean manufacturing process. Or, more correctly, you will implement the system under my guidance. Your boss, Pete, has pledged to provide all the resources you need. Clear enough?"

"Yes, it is. Okay if I use my digital recorder?"

"Good idea."

Tommy scrambled to find his digital recorder buried in the rubble of a desk cabinet and turned it on while Hank waited patiently.

"First things first," Hank said. "Take me for a tour of your plant. Start from receiving and work your way through all of the production departments, finishing with shipping."

Tommy found hard hats and eye protection for Hank and him, and they walked into the plant.

During the plant inspection, Hank's penetrating gaze swept from left to right and back again. He took in the machinery, the inventory, the supervisors and workers, and asked lots of questions, all of them, Tommy was embarrassed to admit, that revealed weaknesses in the manufacturing systems. Every now and then Hank picked up a production order or a quality report and examined it. At the conclusion of the tour they returned to Tommy's office.

"Let's start with the past," Hank said, as he removed his hard hat and sat down opposite Tommy. "That's important. You can't understand what needs to be done without first understanding what's been done before or is being done now. Do you agree?"

"Yes, of course."

"Over the past 30 years," Hank said, "manufacturing managers were led to believe that computerized systems would provide the solution to all of their growth and profit problems. In manufacturing and distribution, systems sophistication was to provide the tools for getting the right material in the right quantity to the right place at the right time. In engineering, computer aided design (CAD) systems were to be the high-tech innovation that improved engineering design and sped the time-to-market process. In sales and service, Microsoft Office was to provide the missing link in effective business communications, while the

Internet's function was to improve order sales capture rates and order processing speed.

"In their efforts to draw closer to customers, many manufacturing professionals lost focus on what should be a company's primary success factor: profitable growth. They pursued total quality management (TQM), enterprise resource planning (MRP and ERP), business process reengineering (BPR), ISO-9001, and Six Sigma, with each respective proponent and guru reassuring manufacturing managers that if they followed their individual programs the bottom-line would take care of itself."

Hank abruptly halted his discourse. "Answer this question, Tommy. Did it?"

Tommy's mouth dropped open. "Did it what?"

"Did all of those wonderful techniques bring unbounded profitability?"

"I ... well, in some cases - "

"The correct answer is they did not! Like most perceived panaceas, each of those techniques was hyped by the business press. Yes, they produced a few success stories, but in general, they contributed little towards helping companies achieve their full potential.

"For a measure of their shortcomings, one needs only to spend some time in a manufacturing facility, especially during the last weeks of the final financial quarter... Like yours, I might add."

Tommy blushed.

"In a typical plant such as this one, you already know that converting the quarterly financial forecast into reality requires overtime, internal and external expediting, last minute on-the-run product changes, and even a little smoke and mirrors."

Tommy's face dropped. "Smoke and mirrors?"

"Don't deny it, Tommy. Denial will only slow your recovery, and may even stop it. You don't want that, do you?"

"No, of course not" Tommy sheepishly admitted.

"Now, where were we? Ah, yes. The inevitable result of all this confusion includes scrap, rework, and warranty costs that damage profitability and quality, and shipment problems that infringe on customer delivery date performance... Am I right so far?"

"I'm embarrassed to say you are."

"Don't blame yourself for what came before you. Companies spent many thousands of dollars in pursuing MRP and ERP and ISO-9001 certification, only to see their business decline due to uncontrolled operating costs that produced non-competitive pricing." Hank turned to Tommy. "So far, so good. Get the picture?"

Tommy said he did.

"Companies have won the Malcolm Baldrige Award for quality and business excellence and subsequently fell far short of achieving growth and earnings expectations.

So, after introducing all these computer systems and more, why is it that most businesses are still struggling to sustain profitable growth and are nowhere close to achieving their full growth and profit potential? Do you know, Tommy?"

"Got to admit, I don't."

"The first reason is simple: The results achieved by any computer system are only as good as the people at the controls and the integrity of the data they provide. The second is more complex: Most manufacturing managers facing major day-to-day problems and constraints adopt a totally reactive management style. Consequently, their time is consumed with applying band aids and finding ways to work around system and process problems, leaving them little or no time to analyze and eliminate the root causes of ineffective systems and processes. How does one turn around such a classic cart before the horse syndrome?"

Tommy stared at Hank.

"Give me an answer, please."

"I guess by changing the way they do things."

"Guessing doesn't count. What's required first is a company-wide, in-depth understanding of the fundamental importance of manufacturing basics, followed by a total commitment to the consistent and tenacious execution of the eight basics of Kaizen Based Lean Manufacturing™... Are you with me so far?"

Tommy nodded. "Computer-based information systems have been one of our problems. Especially our convoluted MRP system."

"Good, then we agree. Like Vince Lombardi, who achieved success by having his team focus on the mastery of football basics, we need to have your manufacturing team focus on the mastery of manufacturing basics."

Hank glanced at his watch. "That concludes our opening session. Today, I spent close to three hours with you, because of the tour. I'll hold to one hour per day for the remaining sessions. Then we start fixing things." He slapped Tommy on the back. "Sound like a plan?"

"Sure does."

"Now, please show me how to return to the lobby."

Chapter Four

The Eight Basic Components of Kaizen Based Lean Manufacturing

When Tommy returned home that night he found the house empty, a note from Jerri saying that she was going on a shopping trip with one of her girlfriends to Los Angeles and wouldn't be back for two or three days.

He called the gym and found out that Jerri's trainer was instructing a client. Next, he called the country club, asking for a tennis lesson. The manager said their regular tennis pro would be out on vacation for the next few days. Would he accept a substitute? Tommy hung up. Bingo! That's all he needed to know.

***

On day two, Hank showed up promptly at 8:00 am. As he did on the previous day, he got down to business right away. "We'll start with an overview of the Kaizen Based Lean Manufacturing™ system. Did you review my lesson from yesterday?"

Tommy's face dropped. "I thought that was all about the past."

Hank sighed. "As I told you, it's difficult to know what to do in the future unless you know what happened in the past. Please review that information tonight, along with our lesson from today."

"Yes si - I mean Hank."

"Now, please pay close attention... Each of the eight basics of lean manufacturing requires proactive planning and tenacious execution that demands leadership above and beyond just satisfying day-to-day accountabilities." Hank stopped and raised his eyebrows questioningly. "Are you with me so far?"

Tommy said he did.

"Some managers can't visualize the benefits of mastering manufacturing basics; others simply can't find the time. Like practicing blocking and tackling in football, it's not exciting, and most football managers, like football players, prefer to run with or pass the ball. But without the tenacious and flawless execution of manufacturing basics, companies will seldom achieve their full growth and profit potentials. Clear enough?"

"Clear enough."

"Very well. Let's take a peek at the eight basic components of Kaizen Based Lean Manufacturing™. We'll start with Information Integrity, the first component. It is not uncommon for front office managers to become disenchanted with computerized system results when time schedules and promised paybacks are not achieved. Acceptable systems results cannot be achieved when systems are driven by inaccurate data and untimely, uncontrolled documentation.

"Next is Performance Management, the second component. Measurement systems can be motivational or demotivational. The individual goal setting of the eighties is a good example of demotivational measurement; it pitted one individual or group against the other and while satisfying some individual egos, it provided little contribution to overall company growth and profit. Today, the balanced scorecard is the choice of manufacturing winners. We'll discuss what it is and how-to in the days ahead.

"The third component is Sequential Production. It takes more than systems sophistication for manufacturing companies to gain control of factory operations. To achieve on-time shipments at healthy profit margins, companies need to replace obsolete MRPII and ERP order launch and expedite methodology with the simplicity of sequential production. The assertion that sequential production works only in high production, widget-manufacturing environments is a myth.

"The fourth component is Point-of-use Logistics.

Material handling and storage are two of manufacturing's high cost, non-value added activities. The elimination of the stockroom and in-process parts queues should be a strategic objective of all manufacturers. And it's time to realize there is much more to increasing supplier contribution to a company's growth and profitability than simply placing purchase orders with the lowest price bidder.

"The fifth component is Cycle Time Management. Long cycle times are symptomatic of poor manufacturing performance and high non-value added costs. Manufacturers need to focus on the continuous reduction of all cycle times for both direct labor and indirect labor tasks. Achieving cycle time management success requires a specific management style that focuses on root cause proactive problem solving, rather than fire-fighting.

"The sixth component is Production Linearity. Companies will never achieve their full profit potential if they produce more than 25 percent of their monthly shipment plan in the last week of the month or more than 33 percent of their quarterly shipment plan in the last month of the quarter. As companies struggle to remain competitive, one of the strategies by which gains in speed, quality, and reduction of costs can be achieved is to form teams of employees to pursue and achieve linear production.

"The seventh component is Resource Planning. One of the major challenges in industry today is the timely right-sizing of operations. Profit margins can be eroded by not taking timely downsizing actions, and market windows can be missed and customers lost by not upsizing the direct labor force when needed. These actions demand tough decisions that require accurate, well-timed, and reliable capacity planning information.

"The eighth and final component is Customer Satisfaction. How do you define that somewhat imprecise term? Customer satisfaction is always in the eyes of the beholder - the customer. Always. Perceptions are what we need to address when it comes to improving customer satisfaction. It does us no good to believe our products and services are best if a customer's perception of their as-received quality and service is contrary. We need real time quality management training and we need to plan and implement proactive projects that breakdown the communication barriers that create invalid perceptions."

Hank stopped and gathered his breath. "Tommy, am I making myself clear? Can you see the distinctions?", said Hank as he sketched the eight components on a sheet of paper.

Information Integrity	Performance Management	Sequential Production
Point-of-Use Logistics	8 components of Kaizen-based Lean Manufacturing	Cycle Time Management
Production Linearity	Resource Planning	Customer Satisfaction

"Loud and clear, Hank."

"One more facet of my argument, Tommy: While many business gurus have identified one or more of these manufacturing basics as important to the successful pursuit of business excellence, the fundamental importance of these Eight Basic Components of Kaizen Based Lean Manufacturing™ has been lost in the proliferation of buzz words and the mania of systems sophistication. It is time to put a hold on unnecessarily complex systems development that causes self-inflicted, day-to-day chaos. In its place, you need to initiate an action learning program for gaining a company wide understanding and acceptance of the importance of the Eight Basic Components of Kaizen Based Lean Manufacturing™. Once you have achieved buy-in and commitment from your employees, aggressive planning and tenacious implementation must follow. In short, let's put the horse before the cart, if you'll excuse my use of such an old trite but true phrase. Such a program will build a solid foundation for redefining and revitalizing your plant's pursuit of growth and profits."

"I've recorded your comments and will study them tonight, Hank... as well as your comments about past manufacturing practices."

Hank cracked a tiny smile. His advice encouraged Tommy and allowed him to entertain thoughts that perhaps his problems can be resolved, after all.

After Hank left for the day, Tommy closed the door to his office and collapsed in his executive chair. He needed to take control of himself, but found it difficult to focus. The unavoidable fact was that he was facing two crises: his career and his marriage. He leaned back in his chair, eyes closed, and took several deep breaths until he felt less uneasy.

Charlene, his secretary for the past year, knocked on the door and entered carrying a cup of Starbucks, French Roast, his favorite coffee. "I thought you could use this about now."

She knew, as well as everybody in the plant, that Tommy was skating on thin ice, and the ice was melting fast. How the grapevine knew this series of meetings with Hank was Tommy's do or die, he couldn't fathom. But the grapevine always knew, always had it right.

"Thanks, Charlene, You're a lifesaver."

A lifesaver she was, an island of composure in a swirling sea of trouble. Whenever Tommy needed to get away for a few minutes, a stolen interlude from the madness of a plant manager's daily life, he spent time with Charlene, talking about mundane matters, just chit-chatting, and walked away calmer, more focused.

"How'd it go today with Hank?"

"The guy's an absolute font of knowledge and wisdom. I'm hoping it will be enough to... " His voice trailed away.

Charlene took his hand and squeezed it. "It's going to be okay, Tommy. You're a good manager. You'll do what needs to be done and succeed." She squeezed his hand, again.

Tommy felt a lump in his throat. He looked up at Charlene and their eyes met and they made that instant connection that men and women have made for aeons and always will make as long as the sun rises in the morning. He had to consciously pull his hand away before he succumbed to temptation and drew Charlene to him and kissed her.

"Look, I've got to make my rounds." His voice was shaky. "I'll be on the production floor for the next hour or so." He started to leave the office but glanced behind at the door. Charlene was standing in front of his desk, her eyes glowing, a soft smile lighting her face.

Chapter Five

The First Basic Component: Information Integrity

"Today," Hank said, "we are going to focus on information integrity, the first component of Kaizen Based Lean Manufacturing™, the underlying pillar of the remaining seven. After all, without reliable data you are unable to know if you're operating to plan. As I've said repeatedly, lean manufacturing objectives cannot be achieved when day-to-day production and manufacturing control systems are driven by inaccurate, untimely, and uncontrolled data and documentation."

Information Integrity	Performance Management	Sequential Production
Point-of-Use Logistics	Eight Basics of Kaizen Based Lean Manufacturing	Cycle Time Management
Production Linearity	Resource Planning	Customer Satisfaction

Hank slapped his knees and rose from his chair. "Let's go out in the plant."

Tommy and Hank entered the plant and stopped at the first machining center. Hank picked up a production order, examined it, and walked up to the machine operator.

He yelled at the operator so he could be heard above the grinding and clanking and roar of machinery. "How often are the part counts right?"

The machine operator laughed at him. "Are you kidding me? The damn ticket[3] is always wrong. Frustrating as hell," he thundered in return. "Either too many parts or not enough. When it's not enough I have to stop production until my supervisor gets it straightened out."

Hank thanked the machine operator and Tommy and he returned to the office.

"Tommy, you see what's happening here?"

"Loud and clear. It's the unreliability of information."

---

3 A production order that accompanies the parts as they travel from station to station within the plant.

Hank nodded in agreement. "Production people like you realize that converting what's specified in the production forecast into actuality unfortunately requires jumping through hoops. Your organization twists itself into knots to fulfil the schedule, and that factor alone contributes to excessive cost, poor quality, and, alas, missed customer shipments. With all the available sophisticated computerized systems at your disposal, Tommy, please tell me, why is it so?"

"Well, if the information provided by the system is unreliable - and I'm using my example here - how can we know the true value of our inventory, and how can we know if we have an excessive amount of parts on hand or not enough parts on hand? I've seen both cases time and time again, just as we saw on the floor today. It's a daily occurrence and a maddening one. You can't control what you don't know about."

Hank smiled and clapped his hands. "Bravo. That's exactly the point. You're catching on."

Tommy beamed in the aura of Hank's approval.

"You see, the answer lies in what's missing and has nothing to do with the quality of the system designs. Like Vince Lombardi, who focused his team on mastering football basics, we need to focus our teams on mastering manufacturing basics. There are eight of those Basics of Kaizen Based Lean Manufacturing™, but when it comes to improving systems performance, Information Integrity is the most important. I call it KBLM Basic #001, Infotegrity: the ability to communicate data and documentation completely, accurately, and in a timely manner. Like blocking and tackling in football, it's not glamorous and few want to do it, but without tenacious and flawless continuous improvement and execution, any implementation of lean manufacturing can never be optimized."

"I'm getting it, Hank. Infotegrity is crucial to computerized master scheduling and MRP computations. Excessive MRP rescheduling of released orders is costly and disruptive and is usually driven by poor input data."

"You nailed it, Tommy. Obviously Information Integrity is one of your key problems, and undoubtedly it will be the first problem we tackle."

Tommy nodded. "Makes sense."

"Let me give you an example. To improve the quality of MRP rescheduling messages, one materials manager I worked with focused on improving the integrity of MRP inputs. She reduced the frequency of their MRP re-generation and implemented a mandatory weekly review and purge and reset of all purchase and production open orders and their status. The results were amazing; reschedule messages were reduced by 85 percent and her planner and buyers gained time to do additional proactive parameter maintenance. Because of increased scheduling stability, there was a significant improvement in both supplier and shop on-time deliveries.

"Here's another example that reveals the importance of Infotegrity. It's an eye-opening result of the cumulative effect of data inputs in a computerized order release and scheduling system such as MRP: There are at least ten data input files that drive such systems with data accuracy indexes varying between 90 percent and 100 percent. Statistically, their cumulative effect (the product of their values) could yield a devastating, order release accuracy of 68.2 percent. That translates into a cumulative 31.8 percent error rate in the order release and scheduling process. In spite of this huge constraint, American ingenuity and energy still gets the job done... but at what cost?"

Tommy made a thumbs down sign. "Those numbers can bring down a manufacturing business."

"Yes, they can, and they have. I've seen it many times."

"Data accuracy is the key, isn't it, Hank?"

"Indeed it is. Although many business gurus have identified data accuracy as important in the implementation of computerized systems, their message has been lost in the mania of systems sophistication. To remain competitive in the future, manufacturers must improve the results gained from their business systems investments. To accomplish that, fine-tuning of Infotegrity is an absolute must. How does a company accomplish this task? Tommy, see if you can tell me how."

Tommy thought about Hank's question. "First simplify databases, making it easy and routine to keep data correct and up to date."

Hank said, "Good start. I'll list the next few: Bulletproof system parameter maintenance, which will help to eliminate mistakes. Then streamline and discipline the product documentation process, focusing on doing it right the first time... Let real time auditing and corrective actions keep information current and correct. Employ the right tools: bar coding, back-flushing, EDI and the internet."

Tommy stuck his hand up like a kid in class. "Here's one I just thought of: establishing the right mindset, the quality of decision-making being dependent on Infotegrity."

"Insightful perception, Tommy. Competition is getting tougher and tougher as each year passes. If you don't want your competitors to close in on your markets, you need to continuously improve product and service quality, increase productivity, lower costs, and increase the speed of new product introductions. To maintain your competitive edge into the future, management's focus must be shifted from systems sophistication to systems Infotegrity. In short, it's time to put first things first. While Information Integrity is no panacea, I'm convinced that a company with simple, unsophisticated systems and a high level of Infotegrity will outperform a company that has sophisticated systems and low Infotegrity. What about those companies that have both? I buy their stock!"

After Hank left, and for the remainder of the day, Tommy hustled around, putting out fires, but more confident now that these sessions with Hank would get his plant moving on the right track. For the first time in several months he felt energized, ready to tackle his problems and resolve them.

***

In spare moments he thought about his secretary, Charlene. He had inherited her from the last plant manager who had left the company for an opportunity elsewhere. She was a slender redhead with a lot of energy whose efficiency professionalized his office. He understood that without her intelligence and dedication to her work (and let's face it - to Tommy), he probably would have tossed in the towel months ago.

He was just beginning to realize how close they had become. Over the course of a year, their boss-secretary relationship had blossomed into something more akin to confidants. Charlene was a single mother, 34 years old, two years younger than Tommy. Her husband, a career Army officer had been killed in Iraq six years ago and Tommy was now her surrogate advisor and friend. Tommy, in turn, cherished the companionship from Charlene he never received from his wife. It wasn't until today that he understood their relationship had moved to the next level. And it frightened him. He had no idea where it would end. But of this he was now certain: his marriage was headed for the rocks.

Chapter Six

The Second Basic Component: Performance Management

Hank and Tommy leaned over a map of the United States spread out over Tommy's desk.

"Tell me, Tommy," Hank said, "how far is it from Phoenix to Las Vegas?"

Tommy quickly calculated distances. "About 287 miles give or take a few miles."

"For purposes of calculation, let's say 300. You might be slightly off, but not significantly for what I'm about to show you."

"Okay, 300 it is."

"Now let's assume you are a salesman and you live in Phoenix. You have the opportunity of a lifetime to make a substantial sale of your company's products to a potential customer in Las Vegas. Your first thought is to fly there but it's possible that flight attendants may be going on strike and that might spread from airline to airline. It's a risk you can ill afford. So you decide to travel by car.

"There is a small problem. The customer has you slotted to make a presentation to him Tuesday at 4:00 pm with competitors making their presentations before and after yours. Normally, for a sales order of this magnitude you would travel the day before. But as luck would have it your company's executive vice president is in town and you're scheduled to have breakfast with him at 8:00 am, Tuesday. You definitely do not want to miss this opportunity. It's a great chance to make a favorable impression. Realistically, you won't finish until 9:00 am, leaving you seven hours to cover 300 miles. Shouldn't be a problem, you tell yourself.

"On Tuesday morning you hit the road 9:30 am, a half-hour late, but you figure you can easily make up the time.

"At 11:00 you've traveled a leisurely 70 miles and decide to take a break and get a coffee. Leaving 230 miles on your journey and five hours to make your 4:00 pm appointment. Not that you're paying close attention to time vs. distance. You're preoccupied with ways to sharpen your presentation.

"At 1:45 pm your car starts overheating. By the time the car cools off and you add water to the radiator, it's 2:30 pm. You glance at the odometer and discover to your chagrin that you have 160 miles to go and one hour and thirty minutes to do it in. That comes to - Tommy, please calculate the miles per hour necessary."

Tommy made a quick calculation. "Wow! 106 miles per hour." He looked up and smiled at Hank. "He's not going to make it, is he?"

Hank shook his head. "Not unless he breaks the law and risks a car crash. In essence, he's missed an appointment for what could have been the largest sale of his career. And don't think for one instant that his boss is not going to be mighty angry. Tommy, what point am I trying to make?"

Tommy thought about it for a few moments. "He should have known how many miles per hour he had to make to meet the 4:00 pm deadline, then check his progress every hour. And when he fell behind, he should have re-calculated the mph needed to make up the loss and checked progress perhaps every half-hour. That way he never would have been caught by surprise after his car overheated."

"Nobody can ever say grass grows under your feet, Tommy. You've nailed it. You see, financial numbers may tell us we're winning the war, but it takes performance management to show us how to focus our energy and efforts to win each of the battles along the way.

"A good friend and coworker, once said, 'You can't control what you don't measure.' Imagine trying to fly an airplane across the country and the cockpit has no dashboard, no gauges, and no idiot lights. You may get the plane off the ground but without performance measurements the chances of getting to where you want to go are slim to none. Business success may not be a life or death situation, but like piloting an airplane, it takes performance measurements to get you where you want to go."

Information Integrity	Performance Management	Sequential Production
Point-of-Use Logistics	Eight Basics of Kaizen Based Lean Manufacturing	Cycle Time Management
Production Linearity	Resource Planning	Customer Satisfaction

Tommy wrinkled his brow. "Just so I understand where you're coming from, what kind of performance measurements work?"

"Good question. As we've already discussed, performance measurement training can turn out to be motivational or demotivational. Using performance standards to pit one worker against the other is certainly demotivational and counterproductive. It creates bitterness among workers and results in poor quality and questionable increases in productivity.

"I agree," Tommy said. "My uncle who worked in a factory in the eighties told me how it spurred competition to the point that workers abandoned quality. Setting one against the other even had the effect of lowering output."

"I have seen that same situation regularly," Hank added. "Today, the balanced scorecard is a performance measurement system that helps companies pursue their key success factors. The scorecard uses both internal and external benchmarking and employs a relevant cascading method of performance goal setting. Achievements are acknowledged and celebrated on a real time basis and not at the traditional annual review.

"For a balanced scorecard process to be motivational it must provide timely and accurate data. Simplicity is a key to the validity of measurements and the tractability of problems to their root cause. Data collection design must employ simple and easy to maintain databases to assure data integrity. When people are trained in this process and are permitted to participate in relevant goal setting, performance measurement can motivate teams to higher achievements, including exceeding growth and profit expectations."

Tommy said, "Okay, I get it, but what elements make up a balanced scorecard?"

Hank slapped Tommy on the back. "You do catch on fast. Let's start with the first: Establish a no status-quo mindset that says if you're not winning, you're losing,

"Two, define company key success factors such as cost, speed and quality.

"Three, identify stretch goals that are relevant to the company's key success factors.

"Four, implement training programs, because when it comes to measurements, education is the pathway to excellence.

"Five, celebrate each goal achieved and raise the bar. Don't wait until next year. That's it. Not hard to understand is it, Tommy?"

"It really isn't. Common sense points the way."

"Indeed it does. But there's still a missing ingredient."

"And that is?" Tommy said.

"For a mature performance management process, benchmarking has become the standard for establishing performance objectives. Yet benchmarking is still one of the most ill-defined management concepts that can mean different things to different people. Our preferred definition comes from Xerox, which describes benchmarking as '... the continuous process of measuring our products, service, and business practices against the toughest competition and those companies recognized as industry leaders.'

"You see, Tommy, the objective of benchmarking is to build on the ideas of others to improve future performance. The expectation being that by comparing your processes to best practices, companies can realize major improvements. One caveat: You should not consider carrying out external benchmarking until you have thoroughly analyzed your internal operations and established an effective system of internal measurement."

Tommy scratched his head. "So what kind of results can you expect when a management team introduces the balanced scorecard?"

"First, employees will become motivated and focused on continuous improvement of their company's key success factors. Second, personal and team achievements will become recognized and rewarded, thereby creating an exciting, winning, work environment. Teamwork will improve and employee retention will rise. Finally, and most important, is company-wide euphoria as bottom line results improve and financial pressures no longer create a stressful and defensive work environment."

"Is that is, Hank?"

"That's it for now. Study up tonight and I'll see you first thing in the morning."

Chapter Seven

The Third Basic Component: Sequential Production

Three days later, Jerri had yet to return home. Tommy was beginning to suspect that she had fled to Daddy after a couple of days of uninhibited sex with her tennis instructor in Los Angeles. He snorted when he imagined Daddy's spoiled princess sitting on Daddy's lap, whining that Tommy may no longer be able to support her in the style to which she had become accustomed.

Tommy seriously doubted that Jerri would reveal those routine afternoon trysts with her tennis instructor and gym trainer. And even if she did, Daddy, without question, would blame Tommy. A no-win situation for Tommy, and he knew it.

Tommy was growing tired of pampering Jerri. He was also sick of hearing the endless comparisons Jerri made between him and her father. Throw a little fear into the mix - Tommy had no doubt that Daddy would gladly have Tommy's legs broken if he pressed the issue - and he was ready to call it quits with Jerri. But carefully, so as not to incite Daddy's explosive temper - although Tommy suspected that Daddy would be happy to get him out of Jerri's life so she could return home permanently; then Daddy could have Jerri all to himself.

Unfortunately, the flare-up with his wife was coming at the wrong time. He was smart enough to realize that he didn't have the resources, either financial or emotional, to fight two wars at the same time. So for now, as he counseled himself, he would place his unsteady marriage on the back burner, and focus on work. Meaning he wasn't about to chase after his wayward wife. Let her stay away for as long as she likes.

***

Tommy and Hank were touring the fabrication area of the plant.

"Look at these lot sizes," Hank said. He picked up several production orders at random. "Lot sizes of thirty, forty, fifty parts and more are the norm." He picked up one production order that showed eighty pieces. "Can you imagine how long it's going to take to get this lot through production, and how many customer shipments will be late because of its slow progress?"

"I know" Tommy admitted. "These lot sizes are a major part of my problem."

"Your plant inventory is glutting the production system. It's comparable to fat and cholesterol in a person's body. Before you know it, those unhealthy ingredients clog up the arteries and the patient collapses." He turned to Tommy. "That's what's happening to your plant."

"What can I do about it?"

"I'll explain, but first a little backdrop... As companies struggle to remain competitive in the 21st century, one of the strategies by which gains in growth and profitability can be achieved is the forming of multi-functional, self-directed work teams. Such teams are needed to focus on optimizing a company's critical success factors such as speed, quality, and costs. A key to effective team dynamics is the development of mutual trust, which can be achieved by eliminating employee and management communication barriers. Employee empowerment and team dynamics are crucial to the design and implementation of sequential production. We'll talk more about this during our final session together."

Tommy sipped his coffee. "Can you give me an example for now?"

"Certainly. As a consultant working with the Spanish truck company Pagaso in Madrid, Spain, I was very impressed with the power of sequential production. Until that time, I was under the misconception that sequential production was reserved for building widgets in a make-to-stock company and could never be implemented in an engineered, made-to-order, OEM manufacturing environment. When I returned from Spain, I directed the conversion of two major MRP, make-to-order, discrete lot size, manufacturing companies into efficient sequential production manufacturers. It's not that unusual. Sequential production is an application methodology that is being adopted by capital equipment manufacturing leaders to gain a competitive edge over their competition.

Tommy said, "I'm still unsure what you mean by sequential production."

"Let's get a cup of coffee and I'll explain." They entered the cafeteria and poured a cup.

Information Integrity	Performance Management	**Sequential Production**
Point-of-Use Logistics	Eight Basics of Kaizen Based Lean Manufacturing	Cycle Time Management
Production Linearity	Resource Planning	Customer Satisfaction

"Let me start this way," Hank said. "Effective shop floor control has proven elusive as companies have upgraded their manufacturing control systems from MRP to MRPII and then to ERP. To capture control of shop floor activities, we need to stop beating a dead horse and start implementing and improving sequential production."

"It comes down to systems, then."

"Look, Tommy, it takes more than systems sophistication for manufacturing companies to gain control of factory operations. To achieve on-time shipments at healthy profit margins, companies need to continuously replace obsolete MRPII and ERP shop order launch and expedite systems with the simplicity of sequential production."

Tommy looked puzzled. Hank noticed it. "This example will help clear up the confusion: Henry Ford first introduced sequential production at his River Rouge operation in 1920. The Ford plant was able to go from receipt of iron ore to casting the engine block, and to shipment of the machined engine block, in a final assembled car in an astonishing forty-eight hours. Ford's success, however, was limited by a manufacturing philosophy that called for the absolute power of a management hierarchy.

"Today the success of sequential production lies in the hands of production workers who use team dynamics to accomplish their work. Product build and test operations content and sequencing, production tools and instructions, logistic layouts, and cycle time targets, are some of the responsibilities of the line worker in today's sequential production environment."

"That's a major transformation" Tommy said. "Let me see if I've got it right. The improvement of speed, quality, and costs are all placed within the responsibility and control of the production worker through team dynamics. Is that what you're saying, Hank?" "That's exactly what I'm saying. Sequential production is neither an inventory control system nor a replacement for MRP. It's an organized and focused assault on production flexibility, speed, quality, and costs. It is a process that requires total employee involvement and participation in the continuous improvement of manufacturing performance. It focuses on cycle time reduction via reduced lot sizes and setup times, preventive maintenance, workplace integrity, visual scheduling, and worker flexibility."

Tommy shook his head in amazement. "That's a mouthful. But I see where you're coming from. Before, all of those tools were the responsibility of management. Now they're vested in the workers doing the job where they truly belong."

Hank smiled and clapped Tommy on the shoulder. "I couldn't have stated it better, my friend. Sequential production tools and techniques include process capability studies, reduced process variances, causal analyses with root cause determination, and relevant corrective actions.

"A lot of work," Tommy said.

"Resulting in a lot of improvement... While starting a sequential production project at the end of the production process and working backwards is good advice, one heavy equipment manufacturer I consulted with began at the front because they could never start a customer's machine build on time. Seems like they always had to wait for the machine's welded base structure to be finished. The excuses for the delay were late shop order releases, raw materials shortages, 'no one told us to start', and it's a huge, complex, time consuming project."

"How did you handle it?" "We decided to break the machine structure build process into a six-station sequential production work cell."

Hank showed Tommy the following chart:

Station #1   Raw materials preparation

Station #2   Sub-assembly welding

Station #3   Frame welding

Station #4   Tank build and installation

Station #5   Manifold build and installation

Station #6   Painting

"The plan was to set the lot size to one and flow the work from one station to the next using visual scheduling and point-of-use logistics (we'll discuss this in the next session). To everyone's surprise and delight, not only did this new production process make life easier for weld shop workers, it increased productivity and improved quality and eventually reduced inventories. But most important, customer lead-times were reduced because machines no longer had to wait for the welded base structure."

Tommy said, "It had to be difficult to train employees, because those changes must have been extensive."

"Smart observation. We discovered that a really good approach to implementing sequential production is to first train all workers in the continuous improvement process (Kaizen) using team dynamics. Next was to select a logical pilot project that's carried out in advance of the rest of the plant roll-out. Project leaders provided an area that was isolated from materials flow in the rest of the plant, but close to production processes similar to the rest. The objective was to gain a quick success before the final roll-out to convince skeptics that sequential production is the way to go."

"That looks like something we can use here," Tommy said. "You think we can do as well?"

Hank winked at Tommy. "As sure as the sun rises every morning and as sure as the government collects taxes from your paycheck. Better believe it."

Chapter Eight

The Fourth Basic Component: Point-Of-Use Logistics

Tommy's days were nothing if not intense. He started work at 6:30 am, was tutored by Hank, and spent the remainder of the day staying on top of his job and making initial plans for his plant's lean manufacturing transformation. He spent his nights studying what Hank had taught him during the day, popped a TV dinner into the Microwave (even when Jerri was home they either ordered in or ate out. Jerri didn't cook), showered, and dropped into bed at 2:00 am, exhausted, and slept like the dead until the alarm woke him at 5:15 am.

This evening when he returned home he found Jerri sitting at her dresser in their bedroom, filing her long, blood-red fingernails and glancing lovingly at herself in the mirror behind the dresser. When she saw Tommy she stopped momentarily, and then resumed filing her fingernails.

Tommy ignored her. He pulled off his suit coat, washed-up, returned downstairs, grabbed a beer from the refrigerator, and sat down at the dining room table where he had piled reports Hank had given him on point-of-use logistics. He sighed and began studying.

Five minutes later, Jerri stormed into the dining room. "Who the hell do you think you are, ignoring me?"

Tommy set down the report he was reading. "I'll tell you who I am. I'm the husband you left behind when you took your toy boy with you to Los Angeles for some screwing and shopping."

Jerri's face turned purple.

"Not that I care, anymore."

"You son-of-a-bitch," she shrieked.

"Just leave me alone, Jerri. I'm not in the mood for any of your tantrums."

Jerri began shaking. Her throat swelled and she was so incoherent she could only spit out a few garbled words.

"Go back upstairs, Jerri, and brush your hair. Unlike you, I've got work to do."

Spit flew out of her mouth, as Jerri, now unthrottled, let loose a stream of invective, culminating in "You bastard, I'm going to tell Daddy how mean you are."

"You do that, Jerri. Go ahead, run home to Daddy. You've been threatening to do it at least once a week for the five years we've been married. Now do us both a favor and just do it!"

After Jerri spun around and rushed out of the room and ran upstairs, Tommy heard their bedroom door slam shut, but not before he heard her scream at him, "Get the hell out of my house."

The house that Daddy built. Tommy had to admit it. The house that Daddy built.

***

"Tommy, you'll never achieve full growth and profit potential, let alone gain the benefits of your supply chain management system, as long as you and other manufacturing professionals continue to talk about value-added supplier partnerships while continuing to treat your suppliers as adversaries."

Although Tommy was upset to the point of distraction about his fight with Jerri, he recognized that now was not the time to focus on his marriage. He forced out any thoughts of Jerri to concentrate on Hank's lessons.

"I hate to admit it, Hank, but you're spot on. When it comes to suppliers we're all talking out of both sides of our mouths. The simple fact is that we refuse to let our suppliers get too close to us."

Hank shook his head sadly. "It's really a shame because material handling and inventory storage are two of manufacturing's high cost, non-value-added activities. The elimination of the stockroom should be a strategic objective of all manufacturers, Tommy, including your own."

Tommy gave a thumbs up. "I agree. We've got parts and materials stocked to the rafters, and that costs money."

"Moving materials to their point-of-use is not a new concept; the auto industry has done it from its beginning, and all industries have had success with point-of-use, low cost hardware. Supply chain development is the key, and it's time to realize that there is much more to increasing supplier contribution to gross profit than simply placing purchase orders with the lowest price bidder. Strategic outsourcing that focuses on getting the right materials, in the right quantity, to the right place, at the right time, and at the lowest total cost, must replace beating-up on suppliers for price reduction alone."

"Amen to that."

"One of my former clients, a manufacturer of electronic component test equipment, in response to its need to increase factory floor space to build a new multi-function tester, decided with my help to convert stockroom space into a production area. It was agreed that none of the new tester parts would enter the remaining stockroom and that all common parts would be relocated to their production areas as point-of-use inventory. The key to making this project a success was the development of a powerful supplier support network that provided timely and innovative point-of-use logistical support."

Information Integrity	Performance Management	Sequential Production
Point-of-Use Logistics	Eight Basics of Kaizen Based Lean Manufacturing	Cycle Time Management
Production Linearity	Resource Planning	Customer Satisfaction

"That had to involve a lot of changes," Tommy said.

"It did. High communications integrity, scheduling flexibility and responsiveness, superior quality, special transportation for materials, storage racks, and a positive continuous improvement mindset were some of the characteristics of the developed relationship. Three years after the project started, this manufacturer was a market leader and most of the credit goes to their supplier development team and the powerful supplier support network that it helped develop."

Tommy signaled Hank to stop while he changed the batteries in his digital recorder. When finished, he signaled Hank to continue.

"In today's competitive business environment, many manufacturing companies are turning to value-added supplier partnerships to achieve the material availability performance that is a requisite to successful point-of-use logistics approach. When a company forms a partnership that performs one of the links in the supply chain, both stand to benefit from the other's success. The power of supplier partnerships is undeniable. To a great extent, they have the best of both worlds: the coordination and scale associated with large companies and the flexibility, creativity, and low overhead usually found in small companies. Suppliers have knowledge and insight but aren't burdened with guidelines from a distant headquarters office. They don't have long forms to fill out and submit weekly reports so they can act promptly, without having to consult a thick manual of standard operating procedures. In an increasing number of industries, value-added suppliers are proving to be fiercely competitive: delivering high quality, competitively priced materials to precise buyer schedule requirements."

"I understand what you're telling me, Hank, but there's one point escaping me, and I believe it's an important point. How do you get buy-in?"

Hank smiled. "You're getting so knowledgeable, Tommy, before I know it you'll be telling me what to do."

Tommy laughed. "Fat chance."

"Look, an excellent way of establishing the partnership relationship is to treat each other as an extension of one's own business. The value-added supplier should look to his partner for services such as special procurement help on capital equipment and training needs and maybe some process engineering or quality engineering assistance. The buying partner, on the other hand, should look to the supplier partner for product development input, cost containment ideas, high quality parts and components, and assemblies delivered the right time, in the right quantity, and at the lowest possible total cost.

"Most business leaders underestimate the depth and breadth of business skills required to initiate and nurture a supply chain management program. Usually, these leaders hold suppliers at arm's length and struggle to keep economic gains to themselves. In fact, organizations often try to weaken a supplier to assure their control of profits. This is ridiculous and it's the first obstacle to overcome if point-of-use logistics is to be implemented. Without a strong supplier network there can be no point-of-use logistics."

Tommy nodded. "I get the point. Makes sense."

"Manufacturing managers in pursuit of point-of-use logistics should be advocates of business integrity, supplier cooperation, free exchange of information, responsive decision making, and supplier profit sharing. Supplier development and strategic outsourcing requires commitment from the top down, accompanied by resources to produce a been-there-done-that team of professionals to make it happen.

"To wrap it up, there can be no effective point-of-logistics approach without supplier partnerships."

Chapter Nine

The Fifth Basic Component: Cycle Time Management

Tommy plopped down in a chair in his secretary's small, crowded office. "I'm frazzled, Charlene. I'm ready for a drink. Care to join me?"

Charlene hesitated. "Well - "

Tommy noticed the pause. "If you don't want to..."

"No, no, I didn't mean that, Tommy. It's just that you've never asked me out for a drink before. I didn't expect it."

They exchanged glances. Tommy smiled, Charlene giggled, and they both started to laugh hysterically.

"We're acting like awkward teenagers," Tommy said between bursts of laughter.

"Oh, this is so funny," Charlene said. She found a tissue in her purse and wiped away tears of laughter.

After their laughter subsided, Tommy said "We're releasing tension."

Charlene nodded. "The stress level has been high around here lately."

The pair remained silent for a few moments, lost in their own thoughts.

Tommy smiled at Charlene. "You never answered my question."

"I would love to have a drink with you."

***

Tommy and Hank walked through the plant to the assembly area. "I want to point out a few things to you, Tommy. "Look at the sequential stations of your assembly line. What's the first thing you notice?"

"If the work is coming off the line."

"Do you mean simply coming off the line or coming off the line as scheduled?"

Tommy blushed. "I see your point."

"Now look at the individual stations. Do you see what I see?"

"I don't know, probably some confusion."

"If you look closely you'll notice a bottleneck operation. It's a bottleneck because assembly operator number one who is feeding assembly operator number two, the bottleneck station, has to stop work until assembly operator number two catches up before she (assembly operator number one) can get back to work. In contrast, assembly operator number three at the station after the bottleneck cannot get enough work from assembly operator number two and also has to stop work. The end result is assembly downtime, low production, high assembly labor costs, and missed customer delivery dates."

"Yeah, I see that."

"Now let's go to the fabrication area."

After they arrived there, Hank said, "You have the same problem here. I've watched a few of your machine and welding work stations. I have to say that many of them are in need of improved fixtures and tooling, and most of them have build sequences that can be combined or eliminated."

"To save money we cut the engineering workforce, and now we're paying the price."

Hank slapped his forehead. "Not a good move. Look at it this way: If your manufacturing team can focus on only one continuous improvement project at a time, then let it be the reduction of total build and test cycle time. There just isn't any other more important success factor to pursue than cycle time management. And if that takes engineering time, so be it."

Information Integrity	Performance Management	Sequential Production
Point-of-Use Logistics	Eight Basics of Kaizen Based Lean Manufacturing	Cycle Time Management
Production Linearity	Resource Planning	Customer Satisfaction

Tommy was busy scribbling notes.

"Long cycle times are a symptom of poor manufacturing performance and high non-value added costs. Manufacturers need to focus on the continuous reduction of all cycle times.

Achieving success requires a specific management style that focuses on proactive problem solving rather than fire-fighting. In this process, management takes on a coaching role, bringing people into the process and supporting them in their efforts to improve productivity, customer satisfaction, and profitability."

"You know," Tommy said, "I was always a proponent of getting workers more involved in their jobs. I can't argue with anything you've said. But how do you go about it?"

"Here's how: Product build and test cycle time is an important element of the total production flow process and provides an excellent focus for a process improvement program. Product build and test cycle time is calculated as the hourly work content through the longest path of the lean manufacturing process. In sequential production, the product build and test cycle time can be calculated by starting at the end of the process and following the longest, cumulative, single path back through the process, regardless of whether it traces the main path or trails off to a sub-assembly path. Many manufacturers have increased their on-time delivery performance and product profit margins by implementing a program of build and test cycle time reduction. The main focus of such a program is the elimination of all non-value-add activities along the path of the product build and test cycle."

Tommy said, "It really does come down to cycle time, doesn't it?"

"It really does, Tommy. In a Harvard Business Review article by Joseph L. Bower and Thomas M. Hout, the authors make a good case for 'Fast-cycle Capability for Competitive Power.' They observe that people in fast-cycle companies think of themselves as part of an integrated system, a linked chain of operations and decision making points that continuously delivers value to the company's customers. In such organizations, individuals understand how their own activities relate to the rest of the company. They know how work is supposed to flow and how time is supposed to be used. Many have used our manufacturing simulation game to change old paradigms."

Tommy put his notebook down and stretched. "How about small companies?"

"In small companies, this way of thinking is usually second nature. Employees find it easy to stay focused on creating value because almost everyone works directly on the products or with customers. Policies, procedures, practices, or people that interfere with getting the product out the door are easy to spot and can be dealt with quickly.

"As companies grow, however, the system-like nature of the organization often gets hidden. Distances increase as functions focus on their own needs, support activities multiply, specialists are hired, and reports replace face-to-face conversations. Before long the clear visibility of the product and the essential elements of the delivery process are lost. Instead of operating as a smoothly linked system, the company becomes a tangle of conflicting constituencies whose own demands and disagreements frustrate the customer. 'I don't care what your job is,' the overwhelmed customer finally complains. 'When can I get my order?'"

"Growth sure has its downside," Tommy said.

"I agree," Hank said, "but only up to a point. Here's an example: Fast-cycle companies, especially the big ones, recognize this danger and work hard to avoid it by increasing everyone's awareness of how and where time is spent. They make the main flow of operations from start to finish visible and clear to all employees, and they invest in this understanding with lean Six Sigma basics training. They highlight the main interfaces between functions and show how they affect the flow of work. They compensate on the basis of group success. And, most important of all, they reinforce the systemic nature of the organization in their operations architecture."

"Then what's the difference between fast cycle companies and others?"

"Good question, Tommy. Fast-cycle companies differ from traditional organizations in how they structure work, how they measure performance, and how they view organizational learning. They use time as a critical performance measure. They insist that everyone learn about customers, competitors, and the company's own operations, not just top management. "

Hank stopped to gather his breath. "Get the picture, Tommy?"

"Loud and clear, but my head is spinning."

Hank laughed. "Don't worry, everything will be crystal clear once we start our implementation."

***

After work, Tommy drove his Buick Enclave and Charlene followed in her Honda Civic. They left their cars in the parking lot behind Silvio's, a quiet neighborhood bar far from the plant.

Once inside they sat down opposite each other in a booth and ordered drinks. Charlene said, "Why this particular bar?"

Tommy blushed, hoping that Charlene wouldn't notice in the muted lighting of the bar. "I didn't know how you might feel about somebody from work seeing us together."

"I don't mind being seen with you, Tommy, if that's what you mean."

"No, I meant the fact that I'm married."

Charlene gazed into her drink. "I have to admit, it does bother me. The last thing I want is to get involved in a broken marriage. I think too much of you to cause you any further unhappiness."

Tommy snorted. "The marriage is over. It's been over for some time." That confession opened the floodgates. For the next twenty minutes Tommy spoke about his marital difficulties: the good, the bad, and the ugly. Especially the ugly. Charlene listened quietly.

When he finished, Tommy leaned back in the booth and closed his eyes. "I just want it to be over," he whispered. "I'm at the breaking point. If I don't focus on getting the plant back in shape, I'm done... done." His voice trailed off.

Charlene reached across the table and squeezed his hand. "Is there anything I can do to help?"

Tommy opened his eyes, leaned across the table, and took both of her hands in his. The connection was electric. "Yes, there is," Tommy said in a trembling voice.

Chapter Ten

The Sixth Basic Component: Production Linearity

"Hank, I'm learning new techniques from you every day, but for the life of me I don't know what production linearity means."

They were walking along the assembly line, witnessing the typical end-of-the-month panic, scheduled orders piling up, supervisors yelling at workers, everybody's nerves frayed from the incessant combat.

"Tommy, let's start with what production linearity isn't, then define what it is. The shipping bottleneck you experience at the end of every month and at the end of every financial quarter - what you're looking at right now - is the antithesis of production linearity. Customer shipments pile up before your last operation, assembly. Before you realize it, assembly is unable to handle scheduled orders. It's comparable to a flexible pipeline that has a bulge at the end of it that's choking off the flow, and nothing is getting out. After a bunch of unscheduled overtime, lousy quality, and sub-standard productivity, the work gets squeezed out, but at what cost? That's what production linearity isn't."

Information Integrity	Performance Management	Sequential Production
Point-of-Use Logistics	Eight Basics of Kaizen Based Lean Manufacturing	Cycle Time Management
Production Linearity	Resource Planning	Customer Satisfaction

"You just described my operation," Tommy said, a trace of bitterness in his voice.

"Once you get work flowing through the plant in planned increments, the last week of the month will be no different than any other week of the month. That's both the objective of and definition of production linearity."

"Nirvana," Tommy said and chuckled. "It's almost unreal."

"Trust me it's real, but like any other desirable objective, you make it happen with good planning, hard work, and the application of commonsense. That's what we'll be discussing today."

"I'm eager to learn about it."

"The most important change that you need to make in your pursuit of production linearity is to go from a monthly to a daily scheduling mentality and reality. Why is linear production so important? It's simple: It's where the money is! Scrap, rework, overtime, and poor quality are all non-value-added costs that increase as a function of the famous hockey stick syndrome. That is, as you delay your production schedule completions toward the end of the month (or worse, toward the end of the financial quarter), there is a tremendous pressure put on your manufacturing organization. This pressure produces shop floor chaos that generates significant non-value-added costs. Yes, I realize you usually end up making the production plan and financial forecast, but that's only because your knights in shining armor come through with a last minute, heroic performance. But, as I've asked before, at what cost? Some companies actually give up 10 to 20 points of their potential gross profit margin because they foster a manufacturing environment that perpetuates the hockey stick syndrome. They unknowingly preserve the syndrome by rewarding their knights in shining armor just as you have."

"What's the hockey stick syndrome?"

"Just what I've been describing, Tommy. The jam-up at the end of the month and quarter, as well as the uneven flow of production orders through the machining and fabrication departments. Picture a hockey stick with the flat portion of the stick on the floor, representing the first three weeks of monthly shipments. Where the hockey stick curves up represents the final week of shipments."

Tommy chuckled. "Pretty clever way to demonstrate the problem."

"It all adds up to money down the drain because of excess inventory, productivity losses, scrap, rework, and unnecessary overtime."

Tommy scratched his chin. "You know, Hank, I'm beginning to see the light. Looks to me like production linearity is one of the major keys to running a top performing manufacturing organization."

Tommy snapped his fingers. "Just thought of this: It's also a requirement for making sequential production a success. Am I not right?"

"You really are, Tommy... Let me tell you a story that illustrates the point. As a young production manager, I was directed to use a huge magnetic board to schedule daily production and monitor production linearity. An early focus on details, corrective actions, and recovery planning became my management style. I held early morning meetings every day to review the previous day's progress as reflected on the magnetic board, and to establish the daily challenges and assign team action items. I became an expert at team dynamics; my employees always knew what they had to do and I provided them with the tools to get the job done. The combination of the magnetic board, the morning meetings, and team dynamics skills earned me recognition as an effective leader and company linear production guru."

"That's quite a story" Tommy said. "But how does it affect computerized manufacturing systems such as materials planning?"

Hank stopped walking and turned to Tommy. "You're really absorbing your lessons. That's an insightful question. Well, to answer it, today many manufacturing managers are still trying to solve their linear production problems by pursuing sophisticated computer software solutions. Most companies use MRPII and ERP manufacturing systems to control their production environments. These systems do not provide a focus on up-front tasks and determination of milestones crucial to linear production. On the other hand, using an old magnetic board in this day and age of computer sophistication may not be an acceptable alternative. A good trade-off might be to develop a simple computer spreadsheet specifically designed to plan critical daily production milestones and to monitor production linearity.

"One company I consulted with used a computer generated spreadsheet. It was the basis for a brief production meeting each morning. After the meeting the spreadsheet was regenerated to update order status and identify the challenges of the day. Not restricted to a big magnetic board in the conference room, their meetings were carried out in the Gemba (factory). Coupled with Management by Walking Around (MBWA) it served as an effective process for identifying and resolving day-to-day shop floor constraints."

"Okay," Tommy said. "I can see that. But what happens to companies that refuse to make the changes?"

"Companies that continue to live with the hockey stick syndrome will never achieve their full growth and profit potential. The shame of it is that it's a solvable problem."

Tommy folded his arms across his chest. "How does a company smooth schedules and achieve linear production?"

"The secret is in keeping daily pressure on the critical path of scheduled tasks and milestones. You need to have the visibility of all critical schedules from day one of the quarter and create team day-to-day awareness and commitment to their timely achievement. Your manufacturing team must become sensitive and proactive in the execution of early production planning details, and they must learn to apply their creativity and energy in a linear style. To be sure, up-front planning and execution can yield amazing manufacturing results and lead to profitability beyond expectations. Now you know your homework assignment for tonight."

Tommy sighed. "My homework assignments keep on building up. It's a steady diet of nights and weekends."

"Don't worry. All of your effort will pay off. Trust me."

***

When Tommy returned home late that night he was unable to unlock the front door. He fumbled with the locks on the garage door and the house's side and back doors, all to no avail.

Frustrated, he dialed Jerri's phone number on his cell phone.

He saw her peer out the bedroom window at him. "How does it feel, smartass?"

"What do you think you're doing, Jerri?"

Jerri giggled. "Kicking you to the curb." She slurred her words.

"You're drunk, and you're not thinking rationally. Now open up the door."

"Not in a thousand years. I want you out of my house and I don't ever want to see your sorry ass, again."

Tommy's voice turned cold. "If I have to, I'll call the police."

"Don't bother, I already have. They're on the way."

Tommy silently swore at Jerri. He knew he was losing control, and he took several deep breaths to calm himself.

Five minutes later a police car pulled up in front of the house. Two police officers warily approached Tommy.

"Are you the resident who called the police?"

"No, I'm not, but I was going to because my wife won't let me in the house. She changed locks on me." Tommy explained the situation

One of the police officers, an older man, was sympathetic to Tommy's plight. He's been in the same situation, Tommy thought. "Sir, I recommend contacting the court for an occupation order. As long as you can prove you're a joint owner the court will grant you access."

"What do I do for now? I need my clothes. She can't keep them from me, can she?"

The sympathetic cop said, "No, sir, she can't. We'll see what we can do." He knocked on the door and yelled "Police, open up, please."

A couple of minutes later the door cracked open and Jerri stumbled out. Tommy noticed somebody behind her in the shadows of the foyer and charged in, pushing Jerri aside. It was Jerri's tennis instructor. Tommy threw himself at the younger man and both tumbled to the floor, thrashing around, uttering curses. The police officers intervened, separating the two. Jerri started wailing, then slipped down to the floor against the door jamb and lost consciousness.

"You should know better than that," the older officer scolded Tommy. "Now I've got to arrest you."

The tennis pro stood and brushed himself off. "It's all right, I don't want to press charges. He thought I was a thief. It was a mistake."

Tommy knew that the tennis pro couldn't afford to have his boss at the country club find out about this incident. They'd boot him out of a job.

"How about her?' one of the officers pointed to Jerri. "Is she okay?"

"Just drunk," Tommy said. "This is not the first time. I'll bring her inside."

"I'll help," the tennis pro said.

The police officers stood by as the two men brought Jerri into the house and set her down on a sofa in the living room. She immediately started snoring.

After the tennis pro left, Tommy gathered his clothes and stacked them in his Buick under the watchful eyes of the police officers. He thanked them and climbed in his car and drove away.

Five minutes later he pulled over to the side of the road and started trembling uncontrollably. He realized how close the end of his career had come tonight and the knowledge shook him to the core.

After the trembling subsided he drove down the road and registered in a motel.

Chapter Eleven

The Seventh Basic Component: Resource Planning

"Tommy, let me ask you a question?"

"Sure thing, Hank."

"How difficult is it for you to adjust your labor requirements to the production forecast?"

Tommy laughed until tears formed at the corners of his eyes. When he gained control of himself, he said, "Sorry, I really don't think it's funny, it's just that you've put your finger on a problem that doesn't seem to have a solution. What you're looking at are tears of frustration."

"I hear you, loud and clear."

"Getting the resources I need is one of my biggest headaches. Because you asked me, Hank, I gather you've run into this problem time and time again."

"I have, and I'll tell you why. The answer might surprise you."

Tommy was wiping his eyes with a handkerchief. "Go ahead."

Hank shook his head in dismay. "The inadequate and untimely availability of resources is a major cause of manufacturers' failures to meet delivery schedules and profit margin forecasts. Believe it or not, material shortages, low productivity, and poor planning are not always the only causes."

Information Integrity	Performance Management	Sequential Production
Point-of-Use Logistics	Eight Basics of Kaizen Based Lean Manufacturing	Cycle Time Management
Production Linearity	Resource Planning	Customer Satisfaction

"Whenever someone asks me, 'Hank, what was the most difficult challenge that you encountered during your career as a production manager?' Without hesitation I respond, 'Convincing our executive leadership of the need to adjust the direct labor work force and then getting their timely authorization to do it.'"

Tommy clapped his hands. "Amen, brother."

"Early in my career, I watched manager after manager fail to get the job done because each didn't have the proper resources in place to deal with the day-to-day challenges of meeting schedules. Most manufacturing managers will tell you that all they need to meet their schedules are the parts, and in many cases they are absolutely correct. However, herein you'll find a business dilemma. When the parts finally do arrive, schedules still aren't met because now the problem is the lack of sufficient production capacity."

"I've been complaining about this to Pete whenever I see him. It's an old issue."

"Most manufacturing managers see the need for adding capacity but are unable to convince top floor executives to hire additional labor because their production operations are generating unfavorable labor variances due to - "

"Tommy finished the sentence. "So-called parts shortages."

"Bingo," Hank said. "The typical response manufacturing managers receive is, 'Why add to the unfavorable labor variance? Resolve your parts shortage problems and then we'll talk about adding people!' It's such a standard executive response it's almost a joke. "Overcoming the parts vs. resources availability dilemma is a prime responsibility of all manufacturing managers and, the inability to do so, is a common cause of their downfall."

Tommy folded his arms across his chest. "Amen, again, brother."

"To deal with the parts vs. resource availability dilemma, most successful manufacturing managers become experts at resource planning. Not in the sense of mastering overly sophisticated computer modeling, but in the practical short-term application of labor needs vs. labor availability. Manufacturing managers will never convince top executives of their resource requirements based on standard financial data because it is always a case of too little too late. Instead, they must gain an in-depth understanding of their capacity and capital equipment requirements, and develop programs and systems that will help convince their top executives that they are in control and that timely action is essential."

"In other words," Tommy said, "short-term resource planning requires that manufacturing managers take control of their own destiny."

"Spot on, Tommy. They must develop effective continuous process improvements to control four critical resource planning activities."

Hank walked to the easel in Tommy's office and wrote these four phrases on it:

> Sales forecasts
>
> People skills
>
> Capacity planning systems
>
> Workload outsourcing

"Let's discuss each of these in turn," Hank said. "We'll start with sales forecasts. One thing we all know about forecasts - they're always wrong."

Tommy applauded and Hank grinned in response. "We manufacturing guys got to stick together," Hank said and winked at Tommy.

Tommy smiled. "Don't you know it!"

"Manufacturing managers must be fully aware of how their portion of the forecast is generated and be cognizant of their past performance to plan. There are two primary techniques to help improve the integrity of forecasts. First, establish time fences to control when products can be added and when they must be dropped from the forecast and, second, develop forecasted Bills of Materials commonly referred to as planning BOMs."

"We develop BOMs routinely," Tommy said, "but the sales manager habitually violates the time fence with last minute or special orders that make us jump through hoops. Sure, I recognize that every company must respond to customer needs, but there's a limit beyond which violating the time fence creates excess cost, missed delivery dates, lower productivity, and lousy quality."

"That's a difficult situation, Tommy. What you have to do is keep track of how many times this occurs, their costs, and then let Pete fight some of your battles with the sales manager."

Tommy grinned, ear to ear. "Gladly."

"Next are people skills. I learned early in my career that people are a company's most precious resource. Manufacturing managers must assure that their employees are on a continuous learning curve or they will become complacent and their skills obsolete. A sound approach to developing and increasing people skills is to continuously perform technical and professional skills assessments and establish an aggressive program to achieve compatibility between needs and availability. The goal is workforce flexibility. There is also a need to develop thinking using outside the box type of skills."

"As I'm sure, you've noticed by now, Hank, that's one of my strengths. I constantly train supervisors and workers in jobs other than their own."

"I have noticed it, Tommy, and I commend you for recognizing its importance... Next is long term capacity planning, normally calculated automatically by materials requirement planning (MRP) and capacity planning (CP) computerized systems. The results can be used as a resource for a home grown manufacturing spreadsheet that forecasts real time labor and skills requirements.

"The final point is workload outsourcing. Manufacturing flexibility, production agility, and reduced product costs are challenges that must be met and achieved by manufacturing managers. Effective outsourcing of projects that focus on a company's non-core business can be worthwhile. To be successful, the program should consist of a target pricing strategy, special material handling techniques, product focused logistics, and strong supplier partnerships."

Tommy mock-wiped his brow and grinned. "Is that all?"

"Just one module left, and we begin implementation."

***

"I know this may sound stupid, but I'm feeling guilty about seeing each other behind my wife's back."

Charlene sighed. "Me, too. I don't like sneaking around."

Tommy and Charlene were sitting side by side in a back booth at Silvio's, their cars parked inconspicuously behind the restaurant, as before. Tommy peered around the bar nervously.

"It's not as if my marriage has any future. It doesn't. It's kaput."

Charlene wove her arm through Tommy's. "Has the court come through with the occupation order yet?"

"Didn't need to. As you know, Jerri let me back in to take my clothes and personal belongings."

"How about Jerri's father? Has he said anything to you?"

Tommy shuddered. "You mean like sending a goon around to break my legs? No, and with any luck I won't hear from him. He wants his daughter back home, so I don't think he'll be too unhappy. He'll get back at me the legal way. He'll lawyer her up and try to strip me of every last cent I own."

"Look at the bright side," Charlene said, tongue-in-cheek, poking him in the side. "You'll get a fresh start."

Tommy sighed. "You know, Charlene, you're joking, but maybe you're right. I've been living so far over my head financially that I never seem to get a moment's peace."

Charlene nestled against Tommy. "Are you sure you don't want to move in with me temporarily?"

Tommy snorted. "Are you kidding? That information would spread through the plant like wildfire. Worse, Pete might find out. No, for now I'll stay at that cheesy motel."

"I never took your boss to be a prude. He isn't, is he?"

"That's not the point. We're in the midst of a major transformation and Pete won't be happy to hear about any distractions. It's a good way for me to get the boot."

Charlene squeezed Tommy's arm. "It's going to work out," she cooed in a soothing tone. "It's always darkest before the dawn." She laid her head on his shoulder.

Darkest before the dawn. Tommy laughed out loud and quickly glanced around the bar to see if any of the other patrons had taken notice. Nobody was paying attention.

They remained in the bar for another hour or so until it got dark, then Charlene followed Tommy to his motel and stayed for a couple of hours before returning home.

Chapter Twelve

The Eighth Basic Component: Customer Satisfaction

"First of all, Tommy, you've made it through to the last session. Congratulations! I've admired your attentiveness throughout the process and your ability to absorb tons of new information, particularly given the fact that you're under the gun. Obviously, you've done your homework."

Tommy grunted. "Under the gun doesn't begin to describe it."

"Not to worry. I've been talking with Pete and he's anxious for you to succeed. He promised to throw his weight behind you and provide the resources to make the lean manufacturing transformation successful."

"That's nice to know, Hank." Tommy shook his head ruefully. "It helps ease the pain."

Hank shuffled around, looking uneasy. "Tommy, it's none of my business, but I've heard about your personal... problems. We've grown close enough so I think I can mention this."

Tommy rolled his eyes. "That damn grapevine! What have you heard?"

Hank blushed. "Maybe I shouldn't have said anything, Tommy, but the rumor mill has it that your marriage is on the rocks. I just wanted to tell you that if there's any way I can help you, don't hesitate to let me know. Sometimes it's good to talk your problems out with somebody not in your immediate circle of family and friends."

Tommy thought his heart was going to explode. He had to ease himself onto a chair before his legs collapsed. "Oh, my God, I don't believe it... Sure as hell, Pete's going to find out."

"That's why I mentioned it. Just so he won't catch you unaware. To the best of my knowledge he hasn't heard, but you know how fast news travels on the grapevine."

Tommy slapped the wall. "With all the problems facing me now, I don't need this." Tommy added to himself: "And I don't need Pete to find out about Charlene and me. That will be the end of both of us."

***

After Hank calmed Tommy, they took up the subject of customer satisfaction.

"The reality of customer satisfaction," Hank said, "is in the eyes of the beholder, the customer. The sooner we realize and accept the customer's perception of our products and services as reality, and accept it as our challenge, the sooner we will earn his confidence and become his permanent supplier of choice."

Information Integrity	Performance Management	Sequential Production
Point-of-Use Logistics	Eight Basics of Kaizen Based Lean Manufacturing	Cycle Time Management
Production Linearity	Resource Planning	Customer Satisfaction

Tommy nodded in agreement. "That really makes a lot of sense. The customer is the ultimate reality and his requirements and wishes should be our bible."

Hank beamed. "Well put, Tommy. Customer satisfaction represents a set of business processes touching on all aspects of the company. Customer satisfaction is a great deal more than the cliché getting close to customers and the motto the customer is always right. Since most companies sell to a variety of customers with varying and even conflicting requirements and wishes, those clichés are too vague, even worthless. We have also found no meaningful business philosophy in the terms market driven and customer oriented. Most business gurus use the phrases interchangeably and have difficulty in defining and communicating their scope and meaning. Successful business leaders go beyond those clichés and strive to provide their customers with products and services under the business philosophy of customer satisfaction."

"Those two terms are just clichés, aren't they, Hank?"

"Indeed they are. Because different customers have different needs, a company cannot effectively satisfy this wide range of needs equally. The most important strategic planning training decision in the pursuit of customer satisfaction is to choose the most important customers. All customers are important, but invariably some are more important than others.

"Collaboration among the various functions is important when pinpointing key target accounts and market segments. This done, sales people know whom to call on first and most often, and managers who schedule production runs know who gets favored treatment; those who make service calls know who rates special attention. If the priorities are not made clear in the calm of planning meetings, they certainly won't be when the sales, production scheduling, and service dispatching processes get hectic."

"How does product and service improvement fit in that agenda? It strikes me that knowing customer requirements is just a start. Without continually tweaking products and services, a company can easily fall behind competitors. Isn't that true?"

Hank's smile radiated. "Tommy, my boy, like I said before, you're not only catching on fast, you're ready to start teaching the subject of lean manufacturing."

Tommy blushed. "Thanks, Hank."

"Let's pursue that line. Customer satisfaction starts with customer selection. However, the next phase you mentioned is just as important. Company executives must gain a thorough understanding of their customers' buying influences and their relevant needs. Such customer information must be communicated by these executives beyond the sales and marketing functions and permitted to permeate every business function. For example, research and development, product design, manufacturing, quality, and field service. When these specialists get unvarnished feedback on the way customers use their products, they can more effectively improve products and production processes. If, on the other hand, market people pre-digest the information, specialists may miss opportunities for improvements."

"In other words," Tommy added, "customer satisfaction must be predicated on continuous improvement."

"And team dynamics and commitment, don't forget those. When one department passes an idea or request to another department routinely without interaction, a manufacturing organization simply can't build the team dynamics and commitment needed for customer satisfaction. Successful new products don't, for example, emerge out of a cocoon in which marketing sends a set of specifications to R&D, and then R&D sends the conceptual design to design engineering, which sends finished blueprints and designs to manufacturing. But joint design and development reviews in which manufacturing and R&D and design employees and other functional specialists share ideas and discuss alternative solutions and approaches - this leverages the different strengths of each party. Powerful internal and external connections make new product development communications clear, coordination strong, and commitment high."

"What you're saying, in so many words, Hank, is that the old way of doing business, serial communication without involvement in anything beyond your functional specialty, no longer cuts the mustard."

"I couldn't have said it better, myself, Tommy. Establishing effective business relationships with key customers is paramount to making it easy for customers to do business with your company. From the shop floor to the front office you must establish one-on-one customer communications that provide real time customer input relative to business relations, product performance, and field service. We must convert those communications to action plans and put forth our best effort to quickly resolve all issues. Let's remember that being nice to customers is just 20 percent of providing good customer service. The important part is designing systems that allow a company to do the job right the first time."

"How does the internal customer fit it? I'm talking about the worker who receives product from a previous workstation? In that sense, all workers are customers, aren't they?"

"I was just coming to that," Hank said. "When we talk about customers, we must also visualize each worker as being a customer of other workers. A worker (the customer) receives his work from another worker (the supplier) and passes his completed work on to the next worker (his customer). This necessitates what I call the one-up, one-down, built-in-quality system."

Tommy gave Hank a thumbs up. "That internal customer concept is exactly what I'm talking about. But what does one-up, one-down mean?" "Implementing a built-in-quality system requires that all workers must be cross trained to perform the job in front of and the job in back of their process. This eventually leads to converting inspectors into productive workers."

"I don't get that, Hank. You still have an inspection department that's after-the-fact."

Hank smiled and shook his head. "Not the way I'm suggesting, Tommy. I'm a firm believer in establishing a quality system that builds quality into the product in lieu of inspecting quality into the product. The days of the inspection department, as we know it, are numbered. Successful manufacturing companies rely on achieving not only built-in-quality but also as-received quality from suppliers. I can point out one very good example: one of my clients. The critical test of their accomplishments came when the CEO "suggested" eliminating the inspection department, but only after developing the ability to build-in-quality. This did not come easy. It took a couple of years. Eventually the company eliminated the inspection department and converted all non-value adding inspectors to value adding workers. Many, including myself, envisioned a disaster. But no such event took place.

"In summary, the increased need to continuously improve built-in-quality processes is a challenge for manufacturers in the 21st century. Companies that get the job done will reach higher levels of quality and will be successful at retaining and adding to their customer base."

"Thanks, Hank. Is this session the last?"

"It is for the eight basic components. But I want an additional session tomorrow morning to discuss self-directed work teams. I also want to go over your implementation plan and timetable before you present it to Pete."

Tommy crossed his fingers. "One more to go, then it's action time. Wish me good luck."

Hank smiled. "I'll be with you every step of the way."

Chapter Thirteen

Making It Happen Through Self-Directed Work Teams

Tommy was riding to work the following morning when his cell phone rang. "Hello."

Pete roared: "Tommy, what the hell is going on?" His boss' anger came across as so intense it was almost palpable. Tommy's heart started racing.

"Pete, I was going to..."

"Of all the goddamn stunts to pull, particularly now..." Pete sputtered.

"Listen..."

"You're starting a major implementation that's going to spell the difference between success and failure of your plant, and to risk it all is plain idiotic."

The bile rose in Tommy's throat. "My marriage is my business, not the company's."

Pete yelled, "Goddamn it, I'm not talking about your marriage. I'm talking about you and your secretary shacking up. So, answer this: is it true? Not that I believe otherwise."

Tommy turned pale and gripped the steering wheel hard. "There's more to the story than what you know."

"Jeez, Tommy," Pete shrieked, "I don't give a rat's ass about the rest of the story. I'm concerned about your attention to the task at hand." Tommy heard Pete groan.

Tommy struggled to maintain calm. "Hank and I are starting the implementation next week. I've already drawn up a step-by-step plan and timetable. You'll see it tomorrow or the day after."

"In the meantime, every member of your organization is buzzing with talk about you and your secretary. That's a major distraction. You've got to stop seeing her, do you understand me?"

There was a deadening silence for a moment. Tommy said, with quiet resolve, "I'm not going to... but I'll make sure we're not seen together."

Tommy could almost feel Pete's icy voice penetrate his ear. "What! Did I hear you right? You're not going to?"

Tommy thought his heart was going to blow out of his chest it was beating so hard. He took a couple of deep breaths. "Listen, Pete, I can handle this lean manufacturing implementation. I've been living it day and night for a couple of weeks now, and I'm primed and ready to go. Besides, Hank will be at my side. My relationship with Charlene has nothing to do with it."

"Nothing to do with it? Jeez, you got a set of balls." Hank groaned again, followed by a chilly silence. "You damn well better be right, Tommy, you better be goddamn right. Screw this one up and you're not only fired, there isn't another manufacturing company that will hire you. This story will follow you wherever you go."

Tommy shuddered. "I'll make it happen, don't worry."

"I don't like it, but I don't really have much choice right now, do I?" Pete's voice was dripping with a combination of bitterness and menace. "Pull you out and who can I put in fast? Nobody... You goddamn well better make sure it happens."

Pete disconnected. Tommy pulled over to the side of the road for a couple of minutes until he regained his composure, and then drove to work.

***

As soon as Tommy arrived at the plant, Hank told him about the grapevine buzzing with the rumor of his relationship with Charlene. Tommy plopped into a chair and described Pete's call. He leaned over and cradled his face in his hands.

"I've messed it all up, Hank."

"Tommy, now listen to me. You haven't messed anything up. We haven't even started the implementation phrase. What you must do right now is to put your personal problems on hold and focus - focus intensely - on the lean manufacturing implementation. Drive any negative thoughts from your mind." Hank gripped Tommy's shoulders. "Will you do this for me, Tommy? Will you do it?"

Tommy straightened up, and a tiny grin lifted the corners of his mouth. "How can I not conform to the wishes of the maestro of lean manufacturing?"

"Great!" Hank gave Tommy a wide grin and rolled up his sleeves. "Let's get to work."

***

"Given highly competitive market conditions, many of today's corporations are struggling to respond to or anticipate market changes in order to remain competitive."

Tommy said, "Always a good thing."

"Yes, always a good thing but too often it creates an unstable and ever-changing environment, where employees are asked to adapt quickly to change. And that inevitably calls for new ways of thinking and developing new skills. In attempting to enable the success of employees, traditional training functions have delivered a variety of interventions to improve performance within their companies. For example: professional development programs, growth templates, training modules, job aids, and so forth.

"However, members of these training groups do not always understand how to assess performance issues. This can cause many glitches within the organization: solutions that do not address inherent problems, initiatives that only partly solve organizational problems, or initiatives that cause problems rather than solving them."

"We suffer from the same disease," Tommy said. "I can't tell you how many training approaches our human resources people have attempted, all with limited success. It does nothing more than confuse our employees, and sometimes has the opposite effect of its intention."

"That's part of the problem, Tommy. The other part and probably the most contentious issue in management training is whether or not to have teams strive for attainable goals or to have them stretch for goals slightly beyond their reach."

"As the old saying goes," Tommy said, "when the going gets tough the tough get going; that kind of management style. I'm familiar with it."

"In my early days I used to argue that setting unrealistic objectives was counterproductive and resulted in a demotivational work environment. I believed that if you set achievable goals, in the long run your gains would be greater than if you establish unrealistic goals. But after working for five bosses, all who established unrealistic goals, I must now agree that setting unattainable goals creates a go-for-it work environment that can produce extraordinary gains in growth and profits."

Tommy's raised his eyebrows. "That's surprising. Changing the way we work is a difficult enough challenge in itself. Employees must be educated, then shown the benefits - not only to the company but to themselves, guided to acceptance, and finally asked for their total commitment. That I understand. But asking them to reach for goals out of their reach?"

"Trust me, it works," Hank said. "When we install the lean manufacturing program, I'll show you. Which brings up the subject of self-directed work teams. As with any organizational innovation, the successful introduction of self-directed work teams involves change. Hierarchies must be flattened, team members must be empowered to make and then implement decisions, new and at times unfamiliar technologies must be adopted, various sources of resistance must be addressed, plans must be clearly communicated, and ownership of the new model of teamwork must be widely distributed."

Tommy grinned. "Another mouthful. Yet everything you just mentioned, Hank, makes sense. Even missing just one of those individual components defeats the purpose of developing self-directed work teams."

Hank rewarded Tommy with a broad smile. "Well put. Isolation, for example, is a habit self-directed work team members can ill afford. The flip side of being left alone to do individual work is that isolation prevents employees from anticipating what lies ahead and from fully understanding the context of the work they're asked to do. Isolated employees feel as if work is coming at them from out of the blue. They find it hard to set, maintain, and balance priorities because they lack a context for making judgment calls. While independence is a fine thing, a desire to communicate and collaborate with teammates is a crucial survival trait in the self-directed work team environment."

Tommy's brow wrinkled. "How about team direction, Hank? How does that work with self-directed work teams?"

"The nature of work in the self-directed work team environment is episodic. Because of the need to handle diverse communications, the most effective team workers are those who can coordinate their efforts based on a shared general purpose and a commonly understood set of priorities. Continuous direction and feedback are luxuries that the leaders of most dispersed teams are not prepared to provide. This is one reason why it is so important for teams to negotiate their priorities and to develop their own sense of purpose and common mission statements."

"I can see that, Hank, but I can also see a problem."

"What problem?"

"While face-to-face meetings, teleconferences, on-line conferences, and e-mail are all effective means to connect, they are neither equal nor completely interchangeable. Just as to a small boy with a hammer, the entire world becomes a nail, to an unsophisticated self-directed work team member, a teleconference call may falsely seem to be the answer to all problems."

"I get your point, Hank said. "Whether this is true or not depends on the nature of their problem and the readiness of team members to use any method as an effective tool. Self-directed work team members need to develop sufficient proficiency with all the tools in their collaborative kit so that technology becomes effectively invisible. This requires initiative, flexibility, and persistence in learning to adapt to technology."

Tommy shook his head. "But that speaks to one so-called type of person. And not everybody thinks the same, behaves the same, or responds to direction the same."

Hank thought about that for a moment. "The self-directed work team environment encourages differences. For example, both introverts and extroverts have an important role to play in self-directed work teams operating across distances, but because of the impact on time zone differences, introverts may enjoy a slight advantage. They can experience a level of satisfying input from an e-mail exchange that an extrovert may find lacking in both spontaneity and warmth. Self-directed work teams need to evolve in ways to sustain both the pace (frequency) and pulse (quality) of their interactions in order to meet the needs of both their introverted and extroverted members. Always a difficult challenge.

"Creating a sense of identity at a distance is one of the greatest challenges that a self-directed work team faces. People who find it easy to identify shared goals with others, to exchange personal history, and to develop common causes with their teammates, can develop a sense of loyalty to multiple teams. Those who find it difficult to diffuse their loyalties may experience themselves as the perpetual loner on any team, a situation that is only exacerbated by time, distance, and technology.

Therefore, to develop identity, you need to focus on the level of interaction that the team must have to accomplish its goals. And then discuss individual accommodations, which may be required for the team as a whole to succeed. There are many ways to bring self-directed work team members together. The starting point is to gauge just how big a distance in terms of habit and preference they need to traverse."

"Hank, I imagine that one of the most pressing problems is the transformation for workers from being directed by supervisors to directing themselves. How do you handle that? It's a substantial change."

"Employees in traditional organizations find that supervisors actively monitor their arrival and departure times, the duration of their rest breaks, their lunch times, the volume of their work, the contents of their reports, and their adherence to approved policies, scripts and procedures. While supervisors have a valid need to over-see their subordinates' work, those same subordinates must not feel that the technologies they use as self-directed work team members are also being used to judge them. If they feel spied upon, the team members' candid communications will be inhibited by concerns about privacy and security. Employees must publish and adhere to policies designed to balance concerns for supervision and the right to privacy of employee communications. Of course, that takes both training and indoctrination."

Hank flipped a page on the easel in Tommy's office. "Let's see if we can write down the essentials of management's new role in the self-directed work team environment."

This is what he wrote:

Management's New Role

- Coaching teams as opposed to directing them.

- Working on longer range strategy instead of putting out fires.

- Supporting teams in their interaction with the larger organization.

- Championing innovative ideas.

- Paying more attention to the technology side of the business.

- Understanding and attending to resource needs.

- Working closer with suppliers and customers.

"Tommy, here's a caution about self-directed work teams from my experience: When organizations see the bottom-line contributions that self-directed work teams can make, there is an understandable tendency to overuse them. Employees on such teams often find themselves assigned too many projects, causing them to experience high levels of stress and burnout. Management must be realistic about the number of teams to which employees are assigned. In addition employees should be allowed to complete current team projects before being assigned to new efforts."

Tommy sat down and exhaled. "Wow, this has been some education for me. I can't wait until we start the implementation."

"That comes the next couple of days after we show Pete our plan... How are you feeling now?"

"Charged up and raring to go."

"You're focused on the plan?

"Totally."

"Glad to hear that," Hank said. "And remember what I mentioned about your personal problems. Back pocket them and focus your entire being on the implementation. With that success under your belt, I'm confident you can resolve your other issues."

The two men stood and shook hands. Tommy choked up and tried to hide it. His final thought was, It's really a gift having a friend and supporter like Hank. Now I can face whatever fate has to offer me with a staunch ally by my side.

Chapter Fourteen

The Turnaround: Defeat Turns into Victory

Tommy gazed in the mirror over the sink in the bathroom of his private office at corporate headquarters. Over the past five years his hair had turned gray and he had the beginning of crow's feet at the corners of his eyes. He looked sadder and wiser yet somehow confident, the latter an adjective he never would have applied to himself five years ago when he had lost his marriage and came dangerously close to losing his job. He marveled at the changes time had wrought and at how capricious fate could be.

Yes, he looked like an executive now instead of the callow youth he had once been (he grinned to himself at the recollection), but getting there had taken its toll.

Was it worth it? he asked his image in the mirror. He had to admit it was. Despite the turmoil, despite the long and brutal hours, despite the exhaustion, and despite the loss of fifteen pounds on a spare frame that couldn't afford it. It had been worth all of that and more. Yet, the battle to survive the corporate fray had left him as battle weary as he had been when he first returned from Afghanistan years ago, a combat hardened Marine. Although lacking the aspect of physical danger, the corporate wars had been just as hard on his nerves and equally as stressful. So had the dissolution of his marriage that ran concurrently with implementation of the lean manufacturing program. There were days when he had been ready to throw in the towel. Yet, somehow, he got up every morning and came to work.

He gave himself a touch-up shave with his electric razor, straightened his tie, pulled down his midnight blue Brooks Brothers suit coat, and walked out of the bathroom into his opulent twelfth floor office overlooking the bustling downtown business district.

Molly, his secretary was standing near his desk. "They're waiting for you in the conference room."

"Is everybody present?"

Molly smiled. "I don't think they dare do otherwise, Mr. President and Chief Operating Officer."

Tommy grinned and shook his head. "Whatever am I going to do with you?"

Molly handed him his morning coffee. "Here's your Starbucks." While he took a few sips she dusted off his suit coat and appraised his look. She gave him the thumbs up sign. "You're ready for battle."

Tommy winked at her and strolled into the conference room.

**

The past five years had been tumultuous, to say the least, and full of surprises. True, the battle had cost Tommy his wife - no great loss - and had emptied his bank account as part of the divorce settlement. And, yes, Jerri's father had threatened to break his legs, but the former gangster knew he stood more to lose than gain, so he had backed off. Especially, since his precious little girl had returned home. His ultimate objective.

The lean manufacturing implementation at Tommy's plant had been a roaring success. Its implementation featured the following changes:

Information Integrity: Tommy and Hank changed all of the major reporting systems with a special focus on the plant's MRP system. They replaced it with a hybrid-MRP system that was easier to use and significantly more accurate than the old MRP system. They also zeroed-in on methods to improve parts counts, production counts, and scrap and rework counts. The transition served as the foundation for the seven remaining lean manufacturing components.

Performance Measurement: The plant scrapped the old performance measurement system that set one worker against the other worker. This mindset had been around for over half a century and was based in part on short-interval scheduling, a technique that measures worker efficiency in small increments of time, often as little as 15 minutes. It was replaced with the balanced scorecard, a more strategic and encompassing measurement system that focuses on team performance.

Sequential Production: Tommy and Hank tackled the burdensome and complex production planning and control system, and using more basic scheduling tools, such as computerized scheduling boards, drove down lot sizes to minimum levels to even the flow of manufacturing orders. Within the first year of the implementation, sequential production helped alleviate end of the month and end of the quarter production bottlenecks (see Production linearity below).

Point-of-use Logistics: As a related activity to sequential production, use of the stockroom and other parts and materials storage points throughout the plant were substantially reduced, and most eliminated. Millions of dollars were removed from inventory and the inventory turn rate doubled.

Cycle Time Management: Management plunged into educating workers and supervisors about identifying and eliminating the root causes of recurring problems, which paved the way for studies by self-directed work teams to reduce production cycle times. Of course, all of this reduced in-process time for orders and helped improve quality simultaneously.

Production Linearity: Tommy and Hank fostered the concept of moving from monthly to daily increments for planning production. This step alone, although difficult to achieve, paved the way for evening out the production flow and eliminating bottlenecks.

Resource Planning: Building on the improvements made throughout manufacturing, Tommy and Hank installed a resource planning module that calibrated resources such as labor requirements with the production schedule and production capacity. This matching step eliminated (or made uncommon) situations where parts and materials were ready for production, but a sufficient number of workers were unavailable to finish production orders on schedule. Conversely, it assured that a drop in the production schedule would require an appropriate drop in labor needs and scheduled parts on a timely basis.

Customer Satisfaction: Although it took a lot of dedicated effort and education, Tommy and Hank were successful in convincing company staff (and especially salespeople who thrashed about wildly when confronted with this concept) that not all customers are created equal. Adaptation of this important principle allowed plant management to focus their efforts on important customers, with less focus on those not as important (application of the 80/20 rule where 20 percent of customers generate 80 percent of sales). The idea of customer satisfaction as a process permeated every line and staff department in the company from design and development through shipping and customer service.

Information Integrity	Performance Management	Sequential Production
Point-of-Use Logistics	Eight Basics of Kaizen Based Lean Manufacturing	Cycle Time Management
Production Linearity	Resource Planning	Customer Satisfaction

***

Looking back on it, Tommy couldn't believe just how lucky he had been. The advent of Hank and his eight basic components of Kaizen Based Lean Manufacturing™ had turned his life around from failure to success, from misery to happiness, from broke to flush. One year into the lean manufacturing implementation, when early signs pointed to a success, Pete, his boss, unexpectedly left the company for a job as executive vice president with a competitor. Based on his plant's successful transformation, Tommy was promoted into his job as vice president of operations. Although relations between Tommy and Pete had not been cordial since the day Tommy disobeyed orders by refusing to give up his girlfriend - Pete, to his credit, didn't stand in Tommy's way when his name came up for promotion.

Tommy appointed his production manager to fill his shoes as plant manager, and immediately, with Hank's help and guidance, he began the lean manufacturing process anew in the remaining plants under his management. Those implementations were just as successful, and the cost savings rolled in.

During this time Tommy became a "comer" in the company, an executive to watch out for. He took on a special project of finding and recommending acquisitions for the company under the direction of the company's CEO.

Because of Tommy's efforts his company acquired three other companies in similar product lines, and all of them added substantially to the bottom line. Four months ago, Tommy's boss, the president and chief operating officer, took early retirement and recommended that Tommy be appointed to take his place. The CEO and board of directors heartily agreed.

And it all had started with Hank and his infallible principles of lean manufacturing. Tommy smiled to himself, remembering how, during his darkest days, Hank had encouraged and supported him. Thanks to Hank, his star is shining brightly.

That evening Tommy met Charlene, his former secretary and now pregnant wife, for dinner at an upscale restaurant in the downtown business district. They were both looking forward to welcoming Tommy, Jr. to the world in a couple of months

END

Appendix

About Bill Gaw
and Business
Basics, LLC

Who is Bill Gaw? And, Why Should We Listen to Him?

Bill Gaw is the founder of Business Basics, LLC, and a been there, done that lean business advocate. He is the developer of seven lean management training packages and eight training modules published to help individuals and companies realize their full growth and earning potential.

Bill is a graduate of the Milwaukee School of Engineering and has earned professional certifications from both the Society of Manufacturing Engineers (SME) and American Production and Inventory Society (APICS). As a former associate professor at San Diego State University, he helped structure and successfully launch their operations management program.

Lean Management Track Record

Bill Gaw's lean management experience spans more than 35 years. During those years, Bill has held positions as a shop expeditor, business planner, buyer, manufacturing manager, vice president, president, and lean-management consultant and educator.

As a lean management business leader he has participated in four successful business turnarounds. In each case, he implemented lean management principles and techniques that brought sanity to the day-to-day operations, eliminated the stress of end-of-the-month scrambling, and created a fun work environment.

At Solar Turbines, as an operations executive, he helped grow the business from $50 million to $500 million while turning losses into profits in the first year of a four-year period. Business systems upgrades and effective implementations were the key to profitable growth.

In Spain, at Pagaso, a Spanish truck company, his parts distribution team was instrumental in turning a huge annual loss into an annual profit, achieving the three-year turnaround objective. Bill designed, developed, and implemented effective lean management techniques based on Kaizen and just-in-time logistic methodologies.

When Eaton Leonard Technology faced bankruptcy, they turned to Bill Gaw. Bill and his operation teams helped achieve profitability in the first year of reorganization. Continuous improvement and motivational performance management provided the driving force for a timely, profitable turnaround.

Palomar Systems wanted greater profit margins and increased sales. Within only four years, Bill's teams increased product profit margin from 32 percent to 55 percent while growing the company from $17 million to a whopping $250 million. This was a classic example of the benefits gained through implementation of lean management principles and techniques, balanced scorecards, and team dynamics.

Bill's Lean Management Training Lab

Using business experiences as a learning lab, Bill methodically researched and tested business ideas, practices, processes, and systems relative to how they contributed to bottom line improvement.

Bill was able to isolate lean manufacturing principles and techniques that are crucial to establishing a solid foundation for personal and company success. Through these experiences, he identified relevant lean manufacturing best practices and documented how to execute them for maximum growth and profit.

Lean Manufacturing Training: Sharing the Knowledge

As an objective of sharing this powerful knowledge with the broadest possible audience, Bill began to write, teach, and coach about the effective implementation and optimization of his lean management best practices. His efforts culminated in the development and publication of seven PowerPoint Plus, training packages and eight training modules. Training options that provide practical e-learning for anyone ... anywhere ... anytime, and can be used for in-house training for all employees.

Now you and your company can benefit from Bill's business knowledge and experiences. The bottom line is this: If your career and your company's bottom line are important, you will benefit from Bill Gaw's lean manufacturing mentoring and coaching. Bill has helped hundreds of individuals and companies fulfil their vision and meet their goals. Now, it's your turn. Want to learn more?

Write, call, or email him at:

Business Basics, LLC

6003 Dassia Way

Oceanside

CA 92056

Phone: 760-945-5596

E-mail: bg@bbasicsllc.com

Website: www.bbasicsllc.com